INSPIRING
WORKPLACES

INSPIRING WORKPLACES

*Creating the Kind of Workplace
Where Everyone Wants to Work*

Michael Kerr

Front cover photograph: Fotosearch
Covers and interior design: Articulate Eye Design, Saskatoon, SK
Edited by: Leslie Strudwick

Printed in Canada

Library and Archives Canada Cataloguing in Publication

Kerr, Michael, 1962 –
    Inspiring Workplaces : creating the kind of workplace where everyone wants to work / Michael Kerr.

Includes bibliographical references.
ISBN 0-9688461-1-4

    1. Quality of work life. 2. Employee motivation.
3. Management. I. Title.

HD6955.K47 2006   658.3'14   C2006-901747-6

Humour at Work Institute™
1-866-609-2640
mike@mikekerr.com
www.MikeKerr.com

- Inspiring Workplaces -

INSPIRE – *v.* 1. to exert a stimulating or beneficial effect upon. 2. to put thought, feeling or life into; to breathe *life* into.

INSPIRATION – *n.* stimulation or arousal of the mind or feelings.

WORKPLACE – *n.* the *environment* in which one works at one's job. (For many people a source of stress, anxiety and despair: *see Dilbert)*

– Table of Contents –

Preface

For a long time I've wanted to pull together ideas and research notes from three filing cabinets and one brain (conveniently, my own) crammed full of assorted, miscellaneous stuff all related to what I affectionately call *inspiring workplaces*. So I've finally done it. In fact, you're about to read it—or at the very least pass it along to your boss as a lovely parting gift.

My motivation for doing this book stems from having worked in a thoroughly uninspiring, dysfunctional work environment. Plus I sincerely hope that no one else goes through what I and many of my colleagues went through, because it really, really, really sucks.

Sadly, too many people are going through what I went through. I speak with too many friends, colleagues and clients who are completely, and take your pick here: uninspired, frustrated, fed up, unmotivated, angst-ridden, bored senseless or completely stressed out. Some even fall into the "all of the above" category.

I made a crucial decision early on about this book—namely that I wanted it to be thorough, but concise; short and sweet. Which meant *not* including specific business examples one might find in numerous other work-related books. This was a tough call, because it's tempting to talk about inspiring companies, such as WestJet Airlines or Southwest Airlines that treat their employees and customers so well, or innovative companies, including W. L. Gore and Associates, which has inspired creativity in their employees, in part, by largely doing away with job titles, hierarchies and, yes, even bosses. There are, thankfully, dozens and dozens of organizations out there—big and small—that are doing many things right, or at least doing *some* things right. There's no question that we can learn valuable lessons from them.

But to keep the book as concise as possible, I tried my darndest to distill hundreds of books, survey results, magazine articles, research papers and conversations with clients down to what I felt was their most important essence—the nuts and bolts and gems and nuggets and basic ingredients of what goes into the pot when you're trying to cook up a truly inspiring recipe for workplace success.

I've set out to achieve two goals with this book. The first goal is to offer a description of what an inspiring workplace looks and feels like, so that you might be so inspired to do whatever you can do to nudge your workplace in the right direction. The second goal is to offer enough practical ideas so that you can use this book as a reference guide, or better yet, buy vast quantities to dole out to your employees, supervisors and colleagues so that they, too, can use it as a reference guide.

The book takes a holistic approach to the workplace because in reality there is not one or even ten things you can scratch off from a "to do" list to achieve inspiration. Creating an inspiring workplace requires a long-term, continuous, disciplined process that necessitates keeping a big picture, holistic view in mind. Creating an inspiring workplace culture is as much about attitude as anything else, and attitude is something that just doesn't register easily on a "to do" list.

There is some overlap here and there. That is very much by design, because the common workplace topics we see presented in books or seminars don't typically separate into convenient, stand alone units. A workplace is like an ecosystem, where all the parts and all the processes are connected to everything else, and so it is impossible to talk about any single aspect of an inspiring workplace without considering the links.

Finally, although I frequently refer to the need for inspiring leadership, I intend for this book to be used by anyone, at any level of an organization. After all, in an inspiring workplace, true leadership is *not* based on position or power, it is present and encouraged at every level within the organization. I believe in people taking responsibility first and foremost for their own lives and their own actions. After all, your own attitudes and behaviours are the only thing that you have 100 percent control over. So although you might feel powerless to affect much change in your workplace, it has been my experience that we all have a lot more influence than we imagine.

And change has to begin somewhere,
so heck, it might as well begin with you.

CHAPTER 1

Imagine... a More Inspiring Workplace

JUST IMAGINE:

Imagine the kind of workplace where *everybody* wants to work: your friends, your family, your competitors and, yes, even your dog want to spend their days there.

Imagine the kind of workplace where people *want* to work hard, where they *want* to contribute their ideas, and where they *want* to do the best possible job.

Imagine the kind of workplace where employees wake up at the start of the work week filled with *passionate enthusiasm* about their work.

Imagine the kind of workplace that truly backs up the phrase: *"Our people are our most important asset."*

Imagine the kind of workplace where people follow their leaders not because they *have* to, but because they *want* to.

Imagine the kind of workplace where people don't want to quit—*ever!*

Imagine the kind of workplace where loyalty between the employee and the organization works *both ways.*

Imagine the kind of workplace where people are *committed* to a *compelling vision.*

Imagine the kind of workplace where employees and customers are *supported*, *respected* and *cared about.*

Imagine the kind of workplace where *loyal customers* become *life-long, enthusiastic advocates* for your organization.

Imagine the kind of workplace where *innovation* and *creativity thrives* and where ideas are welcomed and respectfully considered.

Imagine a workplace where *humanity* rules the ledger.

Imagine if work *didn't feel like work.*

Imagine if work was a *labour of love.*

Imagine . . .

Now some of you may be thinking . . . welcome to Fantasy Island? Is this the start of a John Lennon song? Have the monkeys in my brain taken over the zoo? Do workplaces like this truly exist? Is it even *possible* to create an inspiring workplace?

Creating an inspiring workplace that reaches these lofty heights may seem like an unattainable, utopian dream. But if you don't ever imagine what your vision of an ideal workplace looks like, how will you even begin the journey towards creating a more fulfilling, positive and ultimately, *inspiring* kind of workplace?

I Don't Want to Frighten Any of You, but Imagine the *Uninspiring* Alternative:

Imagine the cost to an organization of *not* attracting the brightest and the best employees.

Imagine the cost of attracting new employees, *over and over.*

Imagine the cost of training new employees, *over and over.*

Imagine the *cost, stress and loss of knowledge, wisdom, creativity and experience* every time an employee quits—and even worse, goes to work for the competition.

Imagine the cost to your workplace when an experienced employee *quits*—but stays right where he or she is.

Imagine the cost of rising employee *absenteeism* rates and work-related *illnesses*.

Imagine the cost of *attracting new customers*, again and again.

Imagine the cost of *not* being creative, of *not* innovating, of *not* keeping up to competitors, of *not* changing; imagine the cost of *stagnating*.

Imagine the toll an unhealthy workplace takes on employees' *mental and physical health*.

Imagine the price employees' *families* pay for the cost of an uninspiring workplace.

Imagine working in an uninspiring workplace for ten, twenty or thirty years and then asking yourself, *"Was it worth it?"*

Imagine the cost to your *soul*.

Imagine if work *felt like work*.

Just imagine . . .

Unfortunately, this scenario is easy to imagine for far too many people. Work-related stress levels are reaching epidemic proportions. Toxic bosses and toxic workplaces are all too commonplace. Like a bad 60s movie, over-stressed and uninspired zombies are taking over too many workplaces. And even if your workplace isn't "all that bad," too many people and too many organizations are settling for mere survival as a benchmark. Too many people are hoping to be voted off their island.

Why are we settling for so little? Shouldn't there be a more rewarding goal than mere survival? Don't you deserve better?

Don't your employees, co-workers, customers and families deserve something more? And is your organization really going to remain competitive over the long run when you're only aiming for *survival?*

Survival might be an okay goal if you are stuck on an island on a reality T.V. show, but it's a lousy way to make your way through life. Survival as a default goal does not motivate or inspire people. And choosing survival as a goal *guarantees* that your company will eventually go the way of the dodo bird.

Organizations that persist in the archaic and ridiculous (feel free to substitute the phrase "unimaginably stupid" if you so wish) belief that people skills and workplace topics such as creativity, humour, communication and inspiration are "soft skills" and somehow trivial, do so at their peril.

Healthy, successful, inspiring organizations and inspiring leaders recognize that it is *not* the cars in the plant, the oil in the ground or the microchips they mass produce that are their most important resource. It's their people.

Let's go even further: People aren't just the most important resource—they *are* the resource. And it's the workplace culture— how people do things and how they treat one another—that forms the foundation for which everything else, *all* of an organization's day-to-day successes, is built upon.

To back up the core belief that people are the most important asset in any organization is not a trite claim. It truly is the difference between success and failure; between thriving and surviving; between an uninspiring and inspiring workplace.

So if you *don't* imagine where your workplace is going and how it's going to get there, if you *don't* consider your people to be your most important resource and if you *don't* consider the human, social and financial costs of an unhealthy, uninspiring workplace, you ultimately risk losing everything.

If, however, you move towards creating a passionate, fun, creative, human and deeply, wonderfully, motivating, inspiring workplace, you stand to gain so much. So the choice seems rather obvious to me. Then again, I'm the author, I have to say this. But, I mean, come on! Get with the program! How could you *not* choose door number one?

What kind of workplace can you imagine
for yourself and your organization?

Still Need Convincing?

Why bother to do anything new and different that will truly have an impact on workplace culture? Do organizations really need to spend precious little time and resources worrying about this stuff?

Here are a few reasons why the answer to those questions is a resounding, enthusiastic: Yes!

1. Life Is Short and We'll All Be Dead Sooner Than We Think

Let's do the math, because a lot of this comes down to basic numbers.

The average life expectancy in a country like Canada or the United States is about 80 years, give or take. And when we die, here's some unsettling news: we're going to be dead for a long, long, time.

As far as any of us can say with any true degree of certainty (with the possible exception of Shirley MacLaine), we all get just one crack at this strange, exasperating and amazing thing called life. And this undertaking we call work, the way we make our way in this world, takes up a huge portion of this short journey.

Most people spend from one-half to two-thirds or more of their waking hours working. If you plow through full time until retirement age, you'll have worked somewhere in the vicinity of 90,000 hours. Work is the single biggest and arguably most important time investment you will ever make. And if you're spending *that much time* doing something, and *that much time* away from your families and friends, then it seems like a more-than-reasonable idea to invest some time, thought and energy into making those hours as rewarding and positive as possible.

This is not to suggest that our work should supercede our families, friends or personal values; to the contrary. But our work *does* have an enormous impact on our life, and it consumes a staggering amount of our precious and limited resources. Because our families and personal life *are* so very important, we owe it to our entire twenty four-hour selves to make sure that something as influential and important as our work is contributing to our lives in as positive a way as possible.

Inspiring workplaces cultivate a humane, positive environment, where people want to spend their limited time, energy and resources.

2. What Do You Do For a Living?

How often have you been asked, "What do you do for a living?" Although I like to answer that question by telling folks that I eat and breathe, we should think about the power behind that phrase. As author Luci Swindoll said, "We have to stop looking at work as simply a means of earning a living and start realizing it is one of the elemental ingredients of making a life."

Our work has an enormous impact on our self-esteem, personal identity and growth as healthy, creative, well-functioning human beings. At its best, what we do for a living represents how we have chosen to make use of our talents to contribute to the betterment of society. Ultimately, when our emotional and spiritual needs are aligned and fulfilled through our jobs, work no longer fees like work.

Inspiring workplaces embody the kind of work atmosphere that lets people be their true, authentic selves. Inspiring leaders nourish their employees' potential and unearth the hidden talents inside their people; they help people to become their best by connecting people with their passions. (Are you getting excited now, or what?)

Inspiring workplaces bring out the best in people so they are able to be the best that they can be and do the best that they can do.

3. Why Should I Work for You?

When it comes to attracting and hiring employees, the outdated paradigm suggests that the prospective *employer* asks the question:

> "Why should we hire you? Prove your worth, show us what you've got, and we'll think about hiring you."

The new, inspiring workplace paradigm suggests that star candidate employees are in a position to flip this question around:

> "Why should *I* come to work for *you*?"

Assuming that organizations want to attract the best, brightest and most creative talent to their workplace, then they need to be prepared to answer that question, because talented, younger candidates who have the mobility and creativity to work wherever they please are asking this question like never before. Furthermore, these crazy young gaffers have less organizational loyalty than ever before—they expect *not* to stay at the same job for the rest of their lives, so hanging on to great employees will become an ever increasing challenge, especially as demographics begin skewing to an older and older population.

The quality of the work environment, the amount of freedom, the potential for creative input and the level of workplace fun are just a few of the workplace issues that the "brightest and best" are interested in. Remember if these folks truly are the best, then they can go anywhere they damn well please! Ditto for all the talented employees already in an organization.

> *The brightest and the best employees are attracted to*
> *a workplace that inspires them. And inspiring workplaces*
> *not only attract good people, they hang onto their*
> *brightest and best employees.*

4. Finding Sanity and Balance in an Insane World

Sooner or later, we're going to figure this one out: stress kills.

Stress is a sanity killer, creativity killer and a productivity killer. Workplace stress can tear families apart, play havoc on marriages, ravage organizations and create really, really, bad hair days. As much as 70 percent of illnesses are thought to be stress-related. And if all that's not enough to stress you out, consider this again, in case you missed it the first time: stress kills.

Inspiring workplaces don't promise the illusion of a stress-free workplace. What an inspiring workplace can do, however, is create the kind of working environment where unhealthy stress levels are minimized, where stress is managed effectively and where people are supported and cared for. Inspiring workplaces take care of the entire person, not just the one that shows up for eight hours a day. And they help their employees maintain a healthy sense of balance in their lives so that they stay healthy and productive in the long run.

Inspiring workplaces are healthy and humane work environments that help nourish a positive balance and perspective in employees' lives.

5. Ideas Inc.

Ideas.

Creativity.

Imagination.

Change.

Innovation.

Survey after survey, business book upon book lauds the growing importance of creativity in the workplace. Employers are seeking creative people like never before, as organizations desperately try to gain the creative edge and foster an environment that will help them innovate and compete on the world stage. Creativity—not intelligence, not working harder, but the application of innovative ideas—will increasingly account for the difference between successful organizations and has-beens. Inspiring workplaces understand that they are in the business of ideas.

Inspiring workplaces are vibrant workplaces where ideas flow freely, where creativity and change is the norm, where passion reigns, where imagination is a valued currency, where smart risks are commonplace and where innovation isn't just talked about—it happens all the time.

6. Inspiring Customer Service

"Would you like fries with that?" just doesn't cut the mustard anymore. Your customers, partners, and internal clients demand more.

In this increasingly global, cost conscious, dog-eat-dingo market-place of ideas and products, wowing people through inspiring service that exceeds basic expectations is increasingly the only way to attract and keep loyal customers. And inspiring workplaces know that to offer inspiring service, they first need to inspire their own employees.

Inspiring workplaces wow their customers with inspiring service: service that treats customers with respect, integrity and humanity. Service that goes above and beyond. Service that inspires life-long loyalty from the customer.

7. In a Bottom-line World, Inspiring Workplaces Rule the Ledger

Forget about the warm and fuzzy group hugs or the feel-good platitudes about life being too short. Forget about a rallying cry for human decency and respecting human values over the bottom line. And forget about basing workplace decisions on humanitarian principles over the almighty dollar. Forget about all that for a moment and let's talk money: dollars and *sense*. Because sooner or later, whether you work in private business or the government, all roads lead to the accounting department.

Here's some great news for the bean counters and shareholders: creating a truly inspiring workplace is a selfish, bottom-line proposition, because inspiring workplaces, by definition, are successful and highly productive workplaces.

If inspiring workplaces attract the brightest employees, allow creativity to thrive, foster highly committed and motivated employees, and are known for their stellar customer service, then it stands to reason that there will be some positive results on the old bottom line. This is also known as the Duh Principle—as in, "DUH!"

Let's face it, this isn't rocket science. It's just the opposite—people science. And what people science tells us is this: people who work in a positive work atmosphere and who enjoy what they are doing perform better. Simply put—people do best what they love doing. And they do best when they are supported and trusted, believe in what they are doing, have pride in what they are doing and work in a fun, engaging, inspiring environment.

Inspiring workplaces are productive,
successful workplaces . . . that work!

> "IF YOU ARE WORKING IN A COMPANY THAT
> IS NOT ENTHUSIASTIC, ENERGETIC, CREATIVE,
> CLEVER, CURIOUS AND JUST PLAIN FUN, YOU'VE
> GOT TROUBLES, SERIOUS TROUBLES."
>
> – *Tom Peters*

CHAPTER 2

Inspiring Vision

Inspiring workplaces have a clear and inspiring vision; one that inspires people at all levels of an organization to move toward a shared, compelling dream of the future.

Now this doesn't mean that you need to save the planet or strive for world dominance in your field to qualify for an inspiring vision. But regardless of what your organization does, to create a truly inspiring workplace there needs to be a compelling reason for employees at all levels of an organization to get up every morning and go to work—a reason that goes beyond simply collecting a paycheque or helping an organization's shareholders make more money.

Money, at a minimum, gets people to show up every morning and warm the benches; a worthwhile vision gets people up off the benches and *moving*. A compelling vision connects hearts with minds to produce amazing results.

This doesn't mean you need to hire a team of consultants and squirrel yourself away for three days of gut-wrenching word tweaking in pursuit of the ideal lofty vision statement to plaster onto your flower-festooned coffee mugs and bumper stickers.

But what it does mean is this:

You really do need a **vision**.

It should be a **compelling** vision.

You need to **connect** your vision with your employees.

You Need Vision

The clichés are too numerous to list, but the simple truism was best articulated by Yogi Berra: "If you don't know where you're going, you'll end up somewhere else."

So where *are* you going? Where is your organization or work team going to be two years from now? Five years from now? Can everyone in your organization answer these questions?

If you don't map out a common path into the woods for everyone to follow, you'll never end up in the forest. A visionless organization ends up lost in the wilderness of confusion and mediocrity. Imagine taking a road trip across the country blindfolded, or taking a family vacation where everyone is driving their own vehicle at different speeds with different directions to different destinations. (If you really want a nightmare scenario, now imagine doing it with my family. But I digress.)

An overall vision guides critical decisions and helps an organization focus on what's most important. It helps employees and clients understand why an organization is doing what it's doing, what it's *not* doing or why it sometimes needs to *change* what it is doing.

A vision of the future also serves as a powerful unifying force, uniting employees at every level in an organization toward one common purpose, ensuring that the entire orchestra is playing from the same, sweet sounding music.

But to create an inspiring workplace full of inspiring music, you need more than just a vision, you need . . .

An Inspiring Vision

Inspiring leaders inspire people with an inspiring vision of where the organization is headed. (Am I a master of simplification, or what?)

Inspiring leaders create a sense of positive urgency, enthusiasm and excitement built around a shared vision that is *compelling and meaningful.*

But before forging onward, let's take a quick side trip and clear up a few definitions, because a mission isn't a vision and a vision isn't a mission.

If you can achieve it by next Friday, it's not a vision. A vision is a dream of the ideal future. No crime. No child poverty. A chicken in every pot. You know it's a vision if, when it's finally achieved, you're not needed anymore (I know, it sounds like a Dilbert cartoon in the making, but it's the truth). The great news is that a vision doesn't have to be long, in fact, the shorter the better. Five or six words is a beautiful thing.

And if you're uncomfortable with the word "vision" then how about just calling it a "Honking Big Really, Really Exciting Goal That Everyone Can Rally Around." (You could always shorten this to an acronym like HBRREGTECRA.)

A mission, on the other hand, spells out why you exist right now. It's why you haul your bones into the office every day. A police force's mission is "to serve and protect," while their ultimate vision might be "no crime" (at which point they'll all be out of business and working as school crossing guards).

A compelling and meaningful mission to go along with your compelling and meaningful vision, is just what the inspiration doctor ordered. The more compelling and simple you make your vision and mission, the better your chances of grabbing the hearts, minds and loyalties of your employees and your customers.

I'm not just talking here about the big overriding global vision your organization has. It's possible to have different levels of visions in a workplace—your particular team or department needs its own vision that unites the troops at a more meaningful level for them. Even individuals can create a vision for their own career, a vision for their own sense of purpose within the organization.

Connect the Dots

You *don't* inspire people by mucking about with words on a coffee mug or framing a nice-sounding vision statement that no one understands. And you sure as heck don't inspire the troops by burying your vision or mission statement in a desk drawer. With his memorable "I Have a Dream" speech, Martin Luther King Jr. didn't inspire folks by sharing his *vision statement* on a PowerPoint slide, he inspired and rallied people behind a *dream* by making an emotional connection.

It's not the words that matter as much as the *meaning behind* the words. Inspiring workplaces know that to really bring a vision to life, a vision can't be a noun, but a verb—an *action* word that implies *doing* something.

Leaders need to model what the vision and mission means and continually guide people toward that vision. Inspiring leaders need to actively demonstrate that they have a *sense of vision*—an ability to see not only out to the horizon, but to see what's lurking beyond.

To create an inspiring workplace, leaders need to link the actions and goals of every department and every employee to the vision and mission so employees:

Understand *why* they need to perform their job in a certain manner.

Understand the *importance* of their job and feel pride in what they do.

Understand *what* it is they need to do.

Understand *how* they connect and contribute to the bigger picture.

Have a reason for going to work that *goes beyond* collecting a paycheque.

Feel *connected* and *appreciated*.

And this includes *everyone.*

The cleaning staff need to know that their role is vital to success because first impressions by clients are critical and long lasting and have a real impact on your mission and vision.

The receptionist needs to understand that how he or she answers the phone *every time* contributes to the workplace vision of what good client service looks, feels and even sounds like.

Team leaders and middle managers need to understand how their leadership behaviour and attitudes contribute to the overall vision.

Frontline customer service staff need to know when they can break the rules—if breaking the rules means that they are contributing positively towards the vision.

To map out a truly inspiring vision everyone needs to be emotionally connected with a vision of where the team *and* the entire company is headed. This isn't simple. It takes a lot of on-going communication. But if everyone is going to take the same road trip together towards the same exciting destination—it is *essential.*

> INSPIRING WORKPLACES CONNECT EVERY PERSON IN AN ORGANIZATION TO A COMPELLING AND MEANINGFUL VISION.

Inspiring Action

1. If you don't have a compelling vision and mission, then create them! What are you *really* in the business of? Besides a paycheque or turning a tidy profit, what is your business? Answer the following question for your organization and *for yourself* at an individual level: why am I getting out of bed every morning?

2. If your vision and mission statements are being used as sleeping aids, then take the time to turn them into short and understandable statements that actually mean something. Hint: If your customers and employees' families can understand them, you're probably on the right track. Another hint: If your vision seems interchangeable with 100 other companies, you're probably on the wrong track.

3. Create a vision and mission for your specific team or department as well; this will help bring the vision closer to home and make it more relevant.

4. Connect the dots: Train all new employees on what the vision and mission actually means in real life. How does it affect behaviour each and every day? How do various jobs link to the bigger picture? Make the training interactive, make it fun and force them (in a nice way) to think about the connections.

5. Keep the vision alive! Find creative ways to communicate it. Post the exciting, inspiring vision and mission on the back of washroom stall doors, above washroom urinals, on computer mouse pads, on the bottom of coffee mugs, on fridge magnets, on key chains, on the website, on paycheque stubs, on t-shirts, on colourful banners. Put the vision to music and create a song, turn it into a poem, produce a fun video, create a mascot or turn it into a story. Make it fun *and* meaningful.

6. Keep the inspiration alive! Remember, the darn thing only means something if it is actually used, so let the vision be your guide—allow it to be your muse. Remind people of it during quarterly meetings. Hold an annual meeting dedicated to keeping the spirit alive. Collect and share stories that illustrate it. Connect it with your values. Link it to employee goals. Use it as a measuring stick and as a motivator.

7. Reflect. If it's true we only value what we can measure, then use the vision and mission to gauge success. In the last year, did you move closer to your vision? Are you *really* doing what your mission says you are in the business of doing?

CHAPTER 3

Inspiring Values

Inspiring workplaces put high value on workplace values.

Values help guide the behaviours and attitudes that determine *how* you travel en route to your destination. Values help ensure that people aren't falling asleep at the wheel, driving recklessly or leaving folks behind at the gas station.

In an inspiring workplace:

Inspiring leaders talk openly about the values they embrace.

Inspiring leaders model the values day in and day out.

New employees understand the organization's values.

Values never change; they're your beacon in a storm.

In an inspiring workplace, the one overarching value that rules the roost, the mother of all values, the value that provides the brightest guiding light in the middle of the roughest weather, is this:

People come first.

Everything else falls out of this simple golden rule: Respect. Trust. Honesty. Creativity. Integrity. Humour. Imagination.

Open communication. Listening. Authenticity. Support. Caring. Service. Leadership. Innovation. Play. Coaching. Teamwork. Team play. Fairness. Openness. Leading vs. bossing. Smart risk-taking. Learning as an investment. Heart. Passion. Guidance. Constructive feedback vs. harmful criticism. Dialogue over monologue. Reasoned debate over autocratic dictation. Tolerance. Loyalty.

Some truly inspiring workplaces place their employees as a higher priority than even their customers. "The customer is number two!" may seem counter-intuitive, yet successful organizations understand that if employees are treated like *they're* the number one priority, then frontline employees in turn will treat the customer with the same sort of respect, loyalty and commitment they receive from their workplace. It pays to keep in mind the old maxim: Most employees won't treat customers any better than they themselves are being treated.

The specific values that guide an organization don't come from a manual or the latest management book. Workplaces don't demonstrate values through periodic "rah rah" team-building events. You can't hold them in your hands or record them on a balance ledger. You can't check them off on a "to do" list. And values don't hang on the wall inside a framed plaque.

Values are driven by the hearts and the souls of employees at all levels in an organization. Values are alive. They are reflected in the way business is conducted at every level. They embody everything an organization *does*, and *how* business is done day in and day out.

Employees know what the values are because inspiring leaders model the values in everything they do. Customers know what your values are because they see them in all aspects of your business. Your values are demonstrated by how you communicate, by the decisions your organization makes, by the way employees and customers are treated and ultimately, by the actions and behaviours of everyone working for your organization.

There's a reason actions speak louder than words. Words merely reflect intentions. *But actions reflect true values.*

For example, when a company tells me that my phone call is very important to them, I often don't believe them, because if my call really was important to them, I'd be talking to a live human being instead of listening to Debbie Boone singing *You Light Up My Life* for the 17th time as I grow old sitting on hold for twenty-five minutes.

If a person takes a cell phone call during a lunch meeting, what is the message that is communicated? Here's one of many possible messages: "I don't even know who is calling but I'm guessing that whoever it is, they're way more interesting than you are."

There are too many organizations and too many leaders that say one thing and do another. They say they value creativity, yet when it comes to trying something new they put up roadblock after roadblock. They "value" trust, but only once they've micromanaged you into a corner. They value openness, yet no one has seen the financial books since the disco era. It's all enough to make you want to start a cartoon about a guy working in a cubicle.

So in an inspiring workplace, some tough questions get asked. If, for example, trust is a core value, do the attitudes and behaviours of all the senior leaders *really* reflect this? How about your rules and regulations around customer service?

If you start using your values as true beacons, then actions will and *must* change to reflect them. *Not* backing up core values is the fastest way to breed workplace cynicism and negativity. (The upside is that employees will understand those Dilbert cartoons a lot better.)

As with a vision, when it comes to defining your values, short and sweet is a beautiful thing. People can't remember ten values, and if there are too many they become meaningless to most people. So pick your top three, four or five values. Then talk about them. Sell them. Post them. Define and explain them through real-life examples. Create stories around them. *Live them.* And never, ever, ever, violate them—*especially* during a crisis, because the values leaders demonstrate during times of chaos shows employees that your values are the real deal and that they serve an important purpose.

What values do you value most?

What values does your organization value?

Are your values aligned with your organization's values?

INSPIRING WORKPLACES MODEL VALUES THAT PUT PEOPLE FIRST.

Inspiring Action

1. If you haven't established a set of core values, then do it. Right now. Go on, I'll give you a day or two to catch up. Keep them short, three to five would be ideal. Include as many employees in the process as possible to gain widespread support for those values.

2. Keep your values front and centre in the hiring process. Hire people who share your organization's values and have demonstrated them in their past jobs.

3. Introduce new employees to your values. Create an interactive training session that makes the connection between the values and the day-to-day behaviours and attitudes of all employees using concrete, real life stories that have happened in the organization.

4. Keep your values alive by communicating them in fun and creative ways: Create humorous posters, write a song, tell life stories that explain them in engaging ways, name corridors after each one, name meal dishes in your employee cafeteria after them, dedicate a month to raising awareness for each of your values, review them during quarterly meetings and never bury them by stuffing them into your desk drawer.

5. During periods of intensive change, take extra time to communicate the importance of your values and stick to them at all costs—they're your beacon in the storm.

6. Create a culture team and assign a senior manager with a title along the lines of "Cultural Ambassador" or perhaps the less intimidating "Grand Pooh Bah of Culture" to help communicate your organizational values.

7. Walk the talk, every day, in every thing you do. Don't underestimate the importance of this.

8. Reflect. In the last year, did your organization live up to its values? Would every employee in your workplace agree that your values really mean something? Are *your* attitudes and actions living up to the values?

CHAPTER 4

Inspiring Goals

Goals are the mileposts along the journey; they are both the drivers and measures of success in an inspiring workplace.

To be inspired, people need compelling goals that stretch their potential, stir their imagination and fire up their engines. Creating truly *inspiring g*oals requires a balancing act because:

> Goals that are mundane or too simple to achieve breed complacency, stagnation, boredom and even stress.

> *While. . .*

> Unrealistic or unsupported goals create anxiety, frustration, stress and a feeling of hopelessness.

> *But. . .*

> Somewhere in between the routine and the unachievable, lie goals that inspire people to reach their fullest potential.

Setting goals that are specific, measurable and that force people to stretch and make the best possible use of their talents is when inspiration becomes the norm. At its supreme best, this is the place where people enter a state of flow, what athletes call "being in the zone." It's a feeling of pure joy where all sense of time is completely lost, where people's skills are perfectly suited to the challenges at hand.

Inspiring workplaces set inspiring goals that help people stretch by:

Matching the right people with the right jobs.

Ensuring people understand what is expected.

Providing the necessary tools and training.

Providing coaching, feedback and support.

Asking employees what they need to achieve their goals.

Removing obstacles in the path of success.

Match the Right People With the Right Jobs

Cubs grow up to be bears. A giraffe is always a giraffe. And acorns grow to be oaks—not elms, not pines, not maples, just oaks. No matter how much we train, prune, nurture, dump fertilizer over them, or will them to be something different, an acorn will always be an oak.

The same, more or less, holds true for people. Inspiring workplaces *allow* bears to remain bears, giraffes to be giraffes and, yes, you guessed it, acorns to be oaks. Of course leaders can train, nurture, coach and inspire oaks to be the biggest, fullest and healthiest oaks they can possibly be, but still, nonetheless, an oak. This has some basic but important implications, namely:

Organizations must hire the right people for the right job.

Managers need to help people discover their hidden talents and passions.

As long as employees are helping achieve the goals of the organization, inspiring workplaces allow them to focus on their strengths and what they are most passionate about.

If you fail at any one of these three, then you are doomed to years of frustration, forever trying to fit the proverbial square pegs into round holes. (I worked with a square peg once, and let me tell you, it's not a lot of fun.) Yet, so many organizations routinely carry out shotgun weddings—hiring, promoting or matching employees with long-term assignments without careful consideration.

No one, save for perhaps Zsa Zsa Gabor or Britney Spears, would ever dream of making the lifelong commitment of marriage after dating for only a week. Yet, in many organizations, people are placed into long-term commitments without investing the proper time and resources at the front end to ensure they have made the best possible match for both parties involved.

So take the time—a whole lot of time if necessary—up front to match folks properly. Inspiration is worth the investment.

People Understand What Is Expected

This sounds simple enough, yet so often employees are left adrift without a complete understanding of what they need to do to achieve the expectations of their supervisor or the organization. We ask people to provide "good customer service," but what does that really look like? How does good customer service translate into day-to-day behaviours and attitudes? Or what do we *really* mean by "exemplary leadership style" or "being a good team player?"

The more clearly a leader can articulate a definition of success and the more clearly they can explain their expectations, the greater the likelihood that goals will be met.

The Tools and the Training to Do the Job

To nurture the talents of your employees you need to give them the training—the *right* training—*and* the necessary tools to do the job properly. Not do it just adequately, but *properly*. This seems like a no-brainer, yet in so many uninspiring workplaces employees chronically complain about the lack of basic training, resources and support to do their job.

In an inspiring workplace, training isn't viewed as an expense or a burden, but just the opposite. Training is considered a vital and necessary *investment* in the people and in the future of the organization. Training serves not only as a tool to enhance productivity, creativity, knowledge and abilities within a workplace, if used appropriately, training is also used as a positive reward and motivator.

Inspiring workplaces create an organization committed to continuous improvement and learning, recognizing that a true expert in his or her field *never* stops learning; a truly inspiring workplace never stops wanting to improve itself.

Coaching, Feedback and Support

Support. Guidance. Advice. Constructive feedback. Coaching. Mentoring. Encouragement. In inspiring workplaces a coaching model replaces the outdated "boss model," where orders are laid down with an iron fist. Or worse still, people are belittled for their lack of accomplishments and motivated through a leadership style dependent on fear, position and intimidation. Many people who quit their jobs are really quitting their bosses, not their workplaces.

In an inspiring workplace, leaders at all levels of an organization coach the best out of their employees. And like any good coach, they listen, observe and provide positive encouragement and constructive feedback that is aimed at helping people be the best that they can be.

Absence of ongoing feedback leads to feelings of isolation, mediocrity and a "so what" attitude amongst employees. Conversely, coaching and feedback that takes place *as needed*— and not just during the annual performance review—ensures continual improvement and sends the message that employees are not alone.

Don't confuse feedback with micromanagement, because one of the most powerful de-motivators are bosses who can't let go of the reins and who gawk like a hawk over the shoulder of every employee. Inspiring workplaces, by contrast, trust their employees enough to allow them ample room to make their own decisions, use their own judgment, and learn from their mistakes. They trust and respect their employees to be the experts in their realm, and treat them as such.

That doesn't mean, however, that employees are left alone in a vacuum. Even the best employees, at any level, require support, encouragement, advice and feedback from time to time, particularly when undertaking more challenging work or when stepping into a new position. Remember, even Wayne Gretzky had a coach during his final season.

And the feedback inspiring coaches offer is always:

Given in a timely manner.

Part of a dialogue.

Constructive.

Specific.

From the heart.

Good coaches ask before they give feedback. They set aside time for a discussion in a neutral setting and create a dialogue, so that open and honest communication can flow in both directions.

And constructive feedback offers comments on observed behaviour only, not attitude. Commenting on a person's attitude sets up a confrontational dialogue, putting people firmly back on their heels in a defensive posture; whereas feedback around behaviour removes labels and finger-pointing, focusing the conversation on observable, specific actions where there is little room for misinterpretation. So rather than suggesting an employee was rude to a co-worker or customer, an inspiring coach discusses the behaviour (use of vulgar language, door slamming, ankle-biting) that was observed.

An effective coach not only points out the observed behaviour, but also offers suggestions for what needs to change, and if necessary, points out both the negative consequences of *not* changing, and the positive consequences associated with the new behaviour. The feedback should always be *future focused*—it's not about rehashing the past.

Finally, constructive feedback comes from the heart, which happens when a coach puts him or herself firmly in the shoes of the person receiving the feedback. The underlying intent of any constructive feedback is always centered on a genuine concern for what is best for both the organization *and* the employee.

Inspiring Constructive Feedback Checklist

- Ask permission before offering any feedback.
- Hold the conversation in a neutral, relaxed setting, free of all distractions.
- Meet at a time when neither party will feel rushed, and when mental distractions are minimal.
- Remember it's a dialogue, not a monologue.
- Focus on observable behaviours, not attitudes.
- Use language such as: "It seems to me . . ." or "I feel like. . ." to remove any feeling of finger-pointing. No one can disagree with your own perceptions.
- Make sure the feedback is specific enough to be useful.
- Keep the dialogue constructive and future-focused.
- If necessary, discuss the negative consequences of not changing and the positive consequences of changing.
- Brainstorm solutions with an open mind so that the dialogue becomes focused on solutions and not blame.
- Offer to help in any way possible.
- Set a date to meet again and follow-up.

What Do You Need to Succeed?

Inspiring leaders ask the following question of their employees all the time: "What do you need from me or from the organization to help you achieve your goals?"

This question serves as a reminder of the changed paradigm at work in a truly inspiring workplace:

Outdated Leadership Paradigm:
Employees serve the leaders
vs.
Inspiring Leadership Paradigm:
Leaders serve the employees; employees serve the clients

When leaders at all levels of an organization shift to an attitude of service, inspiration will follow.

Removing Obstacles in the Path of Success

As important as providing a compelling vision and mission, tools, training and support to help people achieve their goals, it is important to check the path for pitfalls and obstacles in the way. Overburdening employees with too many goals, outdated rules and regulations, autocratic, over-the-shoulder micromanagement, or layers of unneeded bureaucracy are all potential barriers to workers achieving their goals.

Remove the barriers.

Get out of the way.

Let inspiration happen.

It truly is that simple. Honest. Would I lie to you? Of course not.

Does This Mean Never Having to Say You're Sorry?

In an ideal universe people would never be demoted or fired. In an ideal universe we'd always hire the right folks, match them to the perfect job duties and give them the support and guidance they needed to do their work exceptionally well.

The reality is of course that mistakes happen; errors in judgment occur. Even in an inspiring workplace, *especially* in an inspiring workplace, people are accountable for their actions (*not* holding people accountable, in fact, is one of the most effective workplace de-motivators available). If that means demoting or dismissing an employee, so be it.

However, in an inspiring workplace dismissals are done in a timely, professional and respectful manner. Employees that are promoted have a safety net position to fall back to if they end up in a situation where they are mismatched and both the employee and organization ends up suffering.

In an inspiring workplace the person being demoted or let go is given all the support possible and is cared for first and foremost as a human being. He or she is not made to feel like a failure because, if anything, any failure that has occurred has been on the part of the organization. The focus rather is on doing what is right for both the employee and the organization.

A Final Word on Goals and Accountability

While we're on the topic, let's clear up an all too common myth about goals and accountability, shall we?

The fact that some people do not perform as expected in a workplace usually has very little to do with the amount of autonomy they have or with the level of workplace fun. Yet many leaders who rule with an autocratic, controlling style use this thinking to justify their controlling behaviour. Sadly, too many leaders still work from this outdated mindset.

People do not perform as expected because of one of the elements already discussed: the organization hired the wrong person; the employee didn't understand what was expected; the person was put into an assignment before being ready; abilities were mismatched with the job; or someone was not given the proper training, tools, coaching or feedback needed to do the job properly.

With the right set of circumstances, greater workplace autonomy gives people the freedom to be creative and is one of the most powerful motivators there is. Inspiring leaders define the why (through the vision and values) and the what (by setting inspiring goals *with* the employee), and then they get out of the way to let employees use their talents, brains, imagination and creativity to figure out how the job can best be accomplished.

> INSPIRING GOALS IGNITE PASSION, SPARK CREATIVITY AND MOTIVATE EMPLOYEES TO MAKE THE BEST USE OF THEIR TALENTS.

Inspiring Action

1. Review your hiring practices. Are you investing enough time, thought and energy into ensuring that you are hiring the best people for the best job? Are your hiring for attitude and values or *just* skills?

2. Write goals in partnership with the employee. If you are an employee insist on reviewing and developing your goals with your immediate supervisor so that both parties understand and agree on the expectations.

3. Write down goals. The mere act of writing them down substantially increases the chances of completing them.

4. Review goals to make sure they are truly stretch goals. Are they making the best use of you or your employee's talents and passions? If not, what training or changes to the job can be made?

5. Create a training plan that truly reflects the needs of employees and plans for the future.

6. Create a mentorship program that matches veterans with newer employees.

7. Remove all the obstacles in the way of success, such as outdated rules and unnecessary bureaucracy.

8. Offer training for all employees in coaching to ensure that employees at all levels are coaching one another in a positive, constructive manner.

CHAPTER 5

Inspiring Communication

In an inspiring workplace, communication is everything.

In an inspiring workplace, it's easy to speak your mind in a respectful manner. And even easier to be heard. Open, honest, timely and respectful communication happens *all the time*. Real communication isn't an *event;* it's as commonplace as breathing. Inspiring workplaces know that communication isn't the same thing as information—which is only about facts and figures and tends to flow one way—but rather a two-way dialogue that connects at an emotional as well as factual level.

In a truly inspiring workplace:

Actions speak louder than words.

Small talk isn't so small.

Listening is more important than speaking.

Everyone has a voice.

Everyone knows *what's* happening.

Everyone knows *why* it's happening.

How things get said matters.

Actions Speak Louder than Words

"I can't hear what you are saying because your behaviour is so darn loud!" Someone famous said something like this once and I scribbled it down on the back of a napkin because it's so darn true.

Inspiring leaders communicate *all the time*. They know that the most powerful form of communication is action; what a leader *does* and *doesn't do*, has an enormous, lasting impression on every employee. Inspiring leaders lead by modelling the values, actions, habits and attitudes that they want to encourage throughout all levels of an organization. In other words, inspiring leaders know they are "on" all the time.

Again, because it's ridiculously important: Words communicate *intent*, actions *reveal* the truth.

Small Talk Isn't so Small

In an inspiring workplace "small talk" is valued for what it really is. It's the casual conversations in the hallways and elevators, the social niceties that happen first thing in the morning or before a meeting has started and the trivial chitchat in the coffee room that is what builds relationships. Small talk is where people find their authentic voice; it's where people make connections behind their job titles and the masks of professionalism; it's where trust, comfort and openness are created. There's nothing small about small talk, so don't try and stifle it, and better still—create opportunities to encourage it.

Listening Is More Important than Speaking

Inspiring workplaces create opportunities for everyone, at all levels, to be heard. In an inspiring workplace, leaders listen. The organization listens. I mean *really* listens. (And no, I'm not talking about bugging devices.)

In fact, surveys have shown that employees tend to respect leaders more not because they are great *speakers*, but when they are *great listeners.* Inspiring leaders listen for the subtle messages. They listen to gain understanding. They listen for the feelings behind the statements. They create opportunities to listen. Barriers to communication are removed. Dialogue and even healthy debate isn't stymied, in an inspiring workplace it is actively encouraged. Healthy debate is recognized as a sign that people are *alive* and . . .

Passionate!

Concerned.

Engaged!

Open and honest debate also shows that people care enough about their work to become emotionally involved. And involvement leads to commitment.

Recognize that some employees won't be able to articulate their ideas or concerns as eloquently as others. Great ideas and critical information might get lost in a sea of emotions, but inspiring leaders need to listen to all employees, and listen between the lines, regardless of the person's ability to communicate messages clearly or eloquently.

Create opportunities for real dialogue. Foster environments where people feel psychologically safe to be themselves and express their innermost thoughts and feelings.

Everyone Has a Voice

The most effective way to disengage people in a workplace is to *not* give them a voice in their own fate. Inspiring workplaces recognize that for people to feel involved and develop a sense of pride and workplace ownership, they must have a chance to contribute and communicate their ideas and their emotions.

Speaking of Ideas

For inspiration to happen, people need opportunities to contribute ideas. Whether they be small ideas on day-to-day improvements or radical, breakthrough ideas, a worthy idea can come from anyone, at any level of an organization, regardless of their field of expertise. Inspiring workplaces provide opportunities for all employees and customers to contribute their ideas without fear of reprisal, judgment or ridicule.

Numerous surveys suggest that people want to contribute creatively, so much so, that it is a major motivational influence in workplaces. A work environment where people not only feel free to think and voice their ideas, but are *encouraged* to do so, sends the following messages:

"Yes, we *do* pay you to think around here."

"We respect your opinion, experience and input."

"We value you."

And no, installing a suggestion box isn't necessarily the answer. If employees need to slip anonymous suggestions into a box there's a problem—particularly if that is the *only* vehicle a workplace has for gathering ideas. A suggestion box suggests that there isn't a level of trust or comfort that permits people to speak freely. It suggests that there aren't enough opportunities available for employees to freely contribute, or worse, that there are elephants sitting in the corner that no one feels comfortable talking about.

An inspiring workplace offers the chance for everyone to be engaged and to share their thoughts in a positive, supportive climate, even when it's about that elephant that no one wants to mention.

This is *not* to suggest that every idea is a good idea. Nor does it suggest that debates are not welcome. To the contrary, in an inspiring workplace, employees know that they can have their *say*, but not necessarily their *way*.

Vigorous discourse, passionate conversations and positive exchanges of thoughtful ideas are hallmark characteristics of an inspiring workplace. Like a spirited game of volleyball, ideas are regularly served up, bumped around and volleyed back and forth between team players. Ideas are *played* with. If an idea doesn't survive the game everyone on the team understands why and appreciates that *at least their idea was given fair play.* In a healthy debate, no matter how passionate people become, discussions remain focused on the ideas, never on the personalities or people behind the ideas.

Speaking of Emotions

Employees also need opportunities to *express* their emotions in a safe environment so that they don't act *out* their emotions. In an inspiring workplace, people talk openly about their feelings— something that is often discouraged in many conservative workplaces, where logic and cold, hard reason rules supreme. But when you place human beings at the centre of a workplace, then ignoring emotions is as illogical and unreasonable as it can get. People do their best work when their hearts are involved and when logic works in tandem with emotions. To ignore emotions or dismiss gut feelings is a sure-fire recipe for creating a truly uninspiring workplace.

When employees feel unappreciated, angry, depressed or frustrated about an issue, acknowledging their emotions is critical. It can go a long ways towards reducing stress levels, opening up dialogue and finding workable solutions to problems.

Leaders at *all levels* of an organization need to be able to freely express their emotions, as well. Mid-level and senior managers are the least likely to ask for emotional support, yet are often the ones most in need of it. Yet when leaders talk openly and honestly about their emotions, employees are more apt to view them as sincere, trustworthy, approachable, human and, indeed, inspiring.

In an Inspiring Workplace Everyone Knows What's Happening

Ever walked into a lively conversation half way through and felt like a fifth wheel? Or missed the set up part of a joke and wondered why everyone is laughing hysterically? Being left out of the loop in the workplace feels even worse.

Employees need to know what is going on well *before* they hear it from a colleague or read it in the newspaper. Rumours, distrust and insecurities are all bred in a communications vacuum. No one ever complains, "My organization is keeping me *too* informed about what's going on—it's driving me nuts!"

In an inspiring organization all employees have easy access to business plans, financial statements and company reports. Employees are informed of all major company decisions in a timely manner.

Information is power—*when it's generously doled out.* Information fuels creativity—*when it's generously doled out.* Timely and honest information connects people, reduces stress, helps people cope with change and helps employees better serve the client.

And Everyone Knows *Why* It's Happening

Inspiring workplaces don't just keep people informed, they also answer "why":

"Why are we doing it this way?"

"Why do we need to change?"

"Why did she get that promotion?"

Why didn't anyone consider my idea?"

"Why do we need to cut expenses?"

Answering the "why" questions helps ensure people feel connected to the vision and to the broader goals of the organization. Answering the "whys" also demonstrates respect for people and helps employees understand the rationale behind decisions.

How Things Get Said Matters

Finally, inspiring workplaces recognize a basic tenant of effective communication: *"How* you say something usually matters even more than *what* you say."

Translation: appearance, body language, tone of voice, and the vehicle we choose to communicate with all have an enormous impact on how effective we are when it comes to creating inspiring workplaces.

Even when speaking over the telephone, body language and tone of voice has an enormous impact. With interpersonal communications, an engaging physical presence, expressive facial expressions and upbeat tone of voice creates a positive and lasting impression. If you want inspiration to spread, then start by communicating in an inspiring manner yourself.

The medium of communication also has an enormous impact. Although using e-mail to send messages can *seem* very efficient and cost effective on the surface, there are many occasions where face-to-face personal contact is worth the extra effort and time because communication is an *investment*. Too heavy a dependency on e-mail or telephones can cause people to feel alienated and even result in a deterioration in interpersonal communication skills. E-mail messages can easily get misconstrued and offer no chance for immediate feedback or a two-way dialogue. If you want to inspire, there is simply no effective substitute for genuine, warm-blooded, face-to-face, personal contact.

Of course, what we say, our actual choice of words, matters as well. A reliance on buzz words and jargon makes for great Dilbert cartoons, but in the workplace it breeds distrust and cynicism. Healthy, positive language—language that is easy to understand, language that is direct and honest, specific language that paints pictures, language that builds respect, trust and a feeling of good will is the norm in an inspiring workplace. In other words, say what you mean, and heck, while you're at it—mean what you say.

Inspiring workplaces also keep the following inspirational formula in mind:

Information + Entertainment = Inspiration

Boring employees with an annual three-hour meeting is not the way to inspire them to become involved. Which is why many organizations are turning to the creative use of videos or turning their annual reports into musical productions, theatre improvisation skits or mock talk shows as a means of engaging their employees in an entertaining manner.

Inspiring workplaces are also rediscovering the value of stories and storytelling. Pie charts, reams of statistics and stagnant, mind-numbing corporate reports filled with jargon and legalese does nothing to create energy, emotion or excitement. When was the last time you got excited over the number 47? Or when was the last time you enthralled your dinner guests with a colourful pie chart?

Stories are how people best communicate. Stories are the oldest, most moving and the most powerful form of communication. Sharing your organization's stories helps to:

Create a sense of shared history and tradition.

Create heroes at all levels of an organization.

Communicate workplace values.

What kind of stories? Stories about how the company was founded; how early battles were fought and won, or fought and lost. Stories about everyday people doing extraordinary things on a job to make a difference. Inspirational stories of customer service, teamwork or leadership excellence in action. Stories that reveal lessons about value and character. Stories that illustrate the need for change. Stories that connect the heart to the mind.

Turn where you've come from and where you're going into a story, and employees will be inspired to play a role in the next chapter.

In an inspiring workplace people communicate with sincerity, honesty, openness and in an engaged manner that both reflects and contributes to a positive, healthy workplace atmosphere.

Inspiring Action

1. Create opportunities for employees to get to know one another at a personal level. Connecting at a personal level helps build trust and respect and helps people to see one another as real human beings, beyond their job titles and professional personas.

2. Offer training to all employees in interpersonal communication skills. This will become increasingly important as we become more hi-tech, and as those young computer-raised whipper-snappers enter the workforce.

3. Take opportunities to actually tell employees that you not only want, but that you expect them to communicate openly about their ideas, concerns and feelings about work-related issues.

4. Make it easy for any employee to be well-informed. Create a bulletin board system on your website to update employees with new information, send out weekly "what's new" e-mails, hold regular open house forums with senior managers and establish a process that ensures major announcements are communicated to all employees in an effective and timely manner.

5. Take the time to invest in face-to-face communication. This means putting down the phone, backing away from the computer and actually getting up off your seat from time to time. Your workplace— and your body—will thank you.

6. Declare a moratorium on your organization's top ten most overused clichés, buzzwords and acronyms. Buzzwords give people a sense of déjà moo – like they've heard all this bull before. The frequent use of jargon alienates and baffles people,

while increasing levels of mistrust; using concrete, specific and simple language and getting creative with the choice of words clarifies, illuminates and even inspires people.

7. Practice inspiring listening skills: Most people who say they are listening are really just waiting for their turn to speak. Practice active listening and listen for the messages between the lines. Listen to understand. Listen to the emotions behind the words. Listen to what's not being said.

8. Practice inspiring telephone communication. This means never use the speaker phone unless you are doing an impersonation of Darth Vader. Change your voice mail message daily. Be responsive by setting a policy for yourself of returning all calls within 24 hours or by the end of the work day. When speaking on the phone be aware of your body language: standing up helps create a richer tone and gives people more confidence; while smiling dramatically changes the way you sound.

9. Practice inspiring e-mail communication, which means using it at least 50 percent less than you are currently! Don't be lazy with your grammar and spelling—it's an informal medium, but being too informal is unprofessional and uninspiring.

   Practice doing simple things to stand out from the herd. Put in an attention-grabbing, fun subject line so people actually want to hear from you and read the message. Consider the design of your messages: use bullets; leave plenty of white space; watch the overuse of colours. Only send the message to those who need it. Change the subject line in your reply messages so it's more meaningful. Have multiple signature files and use them creatively. Keep your messages short and sweet with a clear purpose in mind and a clear call to action at the end.

(And never accidentally send a personal love letter to all the e-mail accounts in your organization, because it just never ends well.)

10. Make your meetings more inspiring. This could be a whole chapter unto itself, so here's the 60-second version: make your agendas fun and interesting so people actually want to show up; only invite people who really need to be there; have a clear idea of what the purpose of the meeting is; give out door prizes; add a humour break to the agenda; try meeting in different locations other than the BOARDroom; make your meetings efficient, fun, with meaningful discussions and people will be truly inspired. Meetings don't really have to suck the life force out of their participants; they really can and should be inspiring.

11. If you have something to say that requires an actual presentation, then for goodness sakes, make it inspiring. This, too, is a whole book unto itself, but here again is the short version: lose the PowerPoint, or at least the abuse and misuse of it. Save the technical information for handouts, and use the time you have in front of people to share a little personal perspective, humour and inspiration. You don't inspire unless you connect the brains to the hearts, logic to emotions; so again, turn your messages into stories.

CHAPTER SIX

Inspiring Motivation

In an inspiring workplace people feel motivated to perform at their best potential and to continually contribute their ideas, energy and passion.

Inspiring leaders understand that there are no motivational shortcuts. Pep talks, team-building activities and assorted workplace perks all have their place, but creating a highly motivated workforce is not the result of a one-, 10- or 20-times-a-year event. Stoking a fire once every three months is a surefire recipe for burnout. To keep the flames burning brightly, the fire that drives people's passions need to be continuously stoked.

Inspiring workplaces understand these motivational principles:

It starts with a positive work environment.

Carrots (rewards) outperform sticks (threats).

There are different strokes for different folks.

Intrinsic motivators outperform external motivators.

People want to be appreciated and recognized.

Celebrating milestones generates momentum.

Small is beautiful.

Nothing motivates like success.

It Starts with a Positive Work Environment

Assuming you've hired the right people for the right jobs, then happy, positive working environments create happy, positive workers. It doesn't get any simpler than this. Everything begins and ends here. If your workplace environment is poisoned with toxic bosses, brimming with distrust and mired in high levels of stress, then all the motivational perks in the world aren't going to make any difference to the performance of your employees; in fact, they'll backfire and blow up in your face.

Positive work environments are created when:

You hire positive people.

You match people to their best talents
and passions.

People are given clear, challenging goals and
an exciting vision.

People are given the tools and training
they need to do the job well.

Communication is open, honest
and respectful.

Humour and creativity are
allowed to thrive.

The importance of starting with these basics cannot be overstated. You may have a very upbeat, positive work environment, but if someone is put into a position where they feel mismatched and overwhelmed, then obviously motivation will suffer. If employees are not given clear direction, or not given the proper tools and training, then motivation suffers. Motivation also suffers when reward incentives are seen to be unfairly distributed. Even monkeys understand this one.

A research study looked at rewards offered to capuchin monkeys in exchange for simple tasks they performed. To receive a slice of cucumber, the monkey had to give a small rock to the researcher. When their fellow monkeys began to receive greater rewards for those same small rocks, their performance declined. Some refused to take the rewards, even tossing them back. And when monkeys got rewarded for doing even *less* work, well, let's just say the monkeys really went bananas.

By not focusing on the fundamentals of a positive, inspiring work environment, organizations often inadvertently do more to suppress motivation than they do to fire it up. In other words, there are more "off switches" than there are "on switches," so creating a highly motivated workforce is not just about finding the on buttons, it's about minimizing, or better yet, turning off the off switches. These include:

> Internal politics. An absence of open communication. Promoting someone through questionable means. Authoritarian leadership. Idea-squashing behaviours. Rewards not visibly tied to performance. Rumours. Abuse of powers. Micromanagement. Intimidation. Not walking the talk. Lousy coffee.

The list of potential de-motivators is enormous, and it serves as a reminder that ensuring the basics are in place is the first step in motivating employees. After all, what can be more motivating that working in a truly inspiring workplace? In fact, a lot of successful companies don't even think about motivation as a separate workplace issue, because it just happens naturally and because nothing is more motivating than success.

Carrots Out Perform Sticks

Motivation through power, intimidation or threats may work in the short term, but it's motivating through fear. In the long run, inspiring leaders understand that positive rewards out perform negative reprisals when it comes to motivating people and creating a culture of positive energy. Carrots help create a "want to" attitude instead of a "have to" kind of workplace.

Different Strokes for Different Folks

Before talking about some general truths that apply to every workplace, remember the golden rule: Treat everyone the way you'd like to be treated. And then forget the golden rule. Because we're not talking about how *you* would like to be treated, but how different people wish to be treated.

Each employee has his or her own carrot and the key to creating a highly motivated workforce is to find out just what a person's "on switch" looks like. For a lot of people, finding their on switch is mostly a matter of matching them perfectly to the work that makes the best use of their passions and talents. Finding those perfect stretch goals that force people to be engaged, be creative and feel good about the use of their talents is 98 percent of the motivational battle.

Realistically, it can often take years before people unearth their true passions. It may involve lateral transfers, or reshaping goals or job descriptions to allow people the flexibility to move towards jobs that utilize their best talents. Certainly, it takes a lot of dialogue. Leaders need to get to know their people, they need to get to know what drives their crank, what spins their hat, what fires up their engines (okay, I'm running out of metaphors).

Beyond this, when it comes to talking about the traditional motivational perks one thinks of, such as salary incentives, promotions, gifts, or that corner office, once again the golden rule *doesn't* apply. Different employees are driven by different things. While one person might love to be publicly acknowledged, the next person will shun publicity or view it as a shallow incentive. While one employee covets more flexible working hours, another wants more challenging assignments. Where one employee wants to be included on an interesting assignment, another wants to be left alone to focus on a solo project. While one employee seeks a promotion, the next employee has no desire to be promoted upwards, but is instead driven by new challenges and opportunities for growth in the position she or he is already in.

The implications of this are:

Workplaces need to match specific motivators to specific employees.

Workplaces need to offer a variety of motivational levers.

What's the simplest way of finding out what someone's on switch is? Ask. Ask what motivated him or her originally to work in your organization, why this particular field was chosen, and when does he or she feel the best about the job and enjoy it the most?

And the bonus of asking employees for input is that the very *act* of asking employees for input is motivating unto itself.

Intrinsic Motivators Out Perform External Motivators

Inspiring workplaces tap into the intrinsic, internal motivators that drive people's performance, such as pride. External motivators, like money or promotions, can be important, but not nearly as much as the intrinsic drivers of ambition. Money can help attract good quality people and keep employees coming in week after week. For some people, particularly at higher levels of an organization, monetary incentives may be an important motivator. Naturally, no sane person is going to turn down a 20 percent pay raise or keep showing up Monday mornings when the cheques stop coming in.

However, for the most part, money is simply an exchange for the expected work. Money gets people coming in and warming the benches. But to get people up off the benches and moving, to connect to people's hearts and passions, money is a very poor motivator.

Survey after survey reveal that monetary incentives often rank well below other motivators. In fact, where large monetary perks are used as incentives for greater performance, you may inadvertently set up an environment where people feel they work hard because they *have* to, rather than the ideal environment in which they work hard because they *want* to.

External motivators can also, if misused, foster an environment that breeds a survival-of-the-fittest mentality, instead of an attitude based on wanting to do a good job because it's the right thing to do for the team and the organization.

Inspiring workplaces do whatever can be done to tap into people's internal drivers—passion, ambition, creativity, pride—to create the kind of workplace where people want to do their best work and *where the work itself becomes the primary reward.*

Creating a culture of pride is one of the best ways of tapping into those internal motivators. Pride in:

The reputation, mission, history or products of the organization itself.

The performance of the team or co-workers.

An individual's performance and talents.

Inspiring workplaces foster pride by focusing on "what's going right," by telling their organization's success stories and by celebrating the tradition and history of their workplace. Above all else, inspiring workplaces foster pride by remembering that people need to feel valued.

People Need to Feel Valued

When it comes to motivation, what people say they want time and again is simple: They want to be appreciated. They want to be recognized. They want their ideas recognized. They want to know that their work has value and that they are contributing in a positive way.

How do people know they are valued? Promotions and perks may be part of the equation, but often only a small part. Employees in an organization know they are valued when they are asked to be involved in an important project, to join a committee or attend an important meeting. People know they are valued when they are respectfully listened to and when they are entrusted with greater levels of responsibility. They know they are valued when their ideas are given a full hearing, and when they are treated with concern and respect. People know they are valued when they are given latitude to be creative, to make their own decisions and to learn from their own mistakes. And they know they are valued when they are *told they are valued.*

A simple but vital way to value people, is to thank them. Surveys suggest this is, perhaps above all else, what people want more of in their workplaces. Adults need positive feedback as much as children (and, evidently, monkeys). Honest, authentic praise and recognition reinforces positive workplace behaviour, it lets people know they are on the right track and helps create a supportive atmosphere where employees feel proud about their accomplishments. You get the behaviours and attitudes you reward and recognize.

Praise is most effective when it is just that—100 percent positive praise, without any corrective behaviour or critical comments thrown into the mix, because people will just go away remembering the negative critique.

The best praise is:

Sincere.

Heartfelt.

Timely.

Specific.

100 percent
positive.

A handwritten thank-you note, taking time out in a meeting to acknowledge someone, a bouquet of flowers, a small box of chocolates, a fun award or tickets to a movie—the ways to say thanks and give praise through small meaningful gestures, are endless.

Match the Recognition to the Achievement

Common sense suggests you need to match the recognition to the achievement, yet there are horror stories out there. So if someone brought in an additional $5 billion dollars in business, then a coffee mug probably isn't going to do the trick. Likewise, offering someone a free trip to Bora Bora because the photocopier was un-jammed, might be a tad excessive.

Celebrating Milestones Generates Momentum

Inspiring workplaces celebrate continuously. They celebrate the small steps along the journey to larger goals. Creating a culture of celebration reinforces the positives, creates powerful memories, builds traditions and fosters pride.

Inspiring workplaces don't just celebrate work-related victories, but personal milestones and achievements as well. If an employee has done something noteworthy in the community, then organizations should take pride in the fact that they employ community-minded people and recognize those people for their efforts. Celebrating birthdays or similar personal milestones is a simple yet effective way to encourage a greater sense of community within the workplace.

There is no shortage of events worth celebrating, nor is there a shortage of ways to celebrate. If the business you are in is worth doing, it's worth celebrating.

Small Is Beautiful

A recurring theme in this book is the power of small gestures to create an inspiring workplace. It's the small gestures, the simple thanks, the small talk, the small ideas and the small things everyone does *consistently* on a day-to-day basis that contribute most to an inspired workforce. Celebrate and praise the small as well as the big. Take time to do the small gestures that will make someone's day. As business author Alfie Kohn said, "Pay people well and fairly, then do everything possible to help them forget about money."

INSPIRING WORKPLACES CREATE A CULTURE
OF PRIDE, RECOGNITION AND CELEBRATION
AND PROMOTE A POSITIVE WORK ENVIRON-
MENT WHERE PEOPLE FEEL MOTIVATED TO
DO THE BEST THEY CAN DO AND BE THE BEST
THEY CAN BE.

Inspiring Action

1. Provide training for all employees in how to offer positive praise, and use the training to brainstorm ways that employees can support and thank one another on a regular basis.

2. Set up a process for finding out how every employee prefers to be recognized. If you're a front line employee, take the time to let your boss know.

3. Buy a small stockpile of inexpensive thank-you gifts such as coffee mugs, chocolates, funny thank-you cards, office toys and books. That makes it easy to offer someone a small token of appreciation in a timely manner.

4. Create perks and/or celebrations linked to benchmarks or milestones that can be easily measured and seen by everyone.

5. Hold an annual fun awards event. Create fun awards that encourage positive attitudes and behaviours, and throw in some humorous awards as well. Awards might be given out for Rookie of the Year, Best Sense of Humour, Person Least Likely to be Voted Off the Island, Person Most Likely to O.D. on Coffee, or Person Most Likely to Frighten the Photocopier.

6. Recognize personal achievements of employees, whether they be athletic accomplishments or volunteering in the community.

7. Recognize the efforts of the support team. Inspiring workplaces send gifts like flowers or movie tickets to the families of employees, as a way of including and thanking them for their support of a hard-working employee.

8. Create impromptu celebrations and surprise perks, so that employees don't become complacent about the celebrations and *expect* them.

9. Recognize and thank employees in creative ways— have their cars washed or name a cafeteria dish after someone, plant a tree or make a charitable donation in someone's name.

10. Tap into employees' sense of pride by holding an annual open house for the friends and families of employees.

11. Tap into your employees' sense of pride by creating an annual yearbook or scrap book of accomplishments.

12. Participate in charity volunteer activities in the community. This is a great way to build camaraderie and pride, connect people to a meaningful goal and gain support in your local community.

CHAPTER 7

Inspiring Change

In an inspiring workplace, change is the norm.

Change is painful. Change is bad and chaotic and messy. *What a crock.*

In an inspiring workplace, change isn't a chaotic event that swamps an organization every ten years. Change is the norm, it happens *all the time* as people strive to find better or newer ways of doing things. I'm not talking about change just for change's sake, or changing the organizational structure each time a new leader comes in so they can put their own stamp on things. Those kinds of unnecessary changes can quickly create chaos and divert organizations away from their mission at hand.

By including employees in the process, change in an inspiring workplace isn't something that happens *to* them, it happens *with* the employees who are *part* of the change process and who can champion and drive necessary changes. Employees at all levels are encouraged to adopt an entrepreneurial attitude towards their work.

Of course, some change will happen from time to time, that, from necessity, will be driven from senior levels. When these changes do occur, they should be managed in such a way that employees don't feel threatened, insecure or stressed about the uncertainty around them. Above all else, in inspiring workplaces a premium is placed on effective communication so that everyone understands:

Why the change is necessary.

What the positive consequences of changing are.

What's *not* going to change.

What values will guide the change.

What training and resources will be available.

How the change will be evaluated.

What happens if the change doesn't work.

Why Change?

When organizational changes are driven from higher levels, people need to be told clearly *why* things must change. They must be sold on the need for change. This means managers and leaders at all levels of an organization need to spend a lot of time investing in an on-going dialogue with their employees. During intensive periods of change, as much as 80 percent of a manager's time may be tied up in communicating with employees. Inspiring leaders understand that this amount of communication isn't a burden, rather it's a sound investment that will help reduce stress levels and facilitate an easier transition period.

While championing the change, inspiring leaders allow for open dialogue so that employees can voice their concerns—both real and imagined—over the changes that are taking place around them. Opportunities for employees to become involved in the process need to be fully utilized. Meetings, informal coffee gatherings, newsletters, videos, presentations and even social celebrations are all thrown into the mix to make sure employees feel included and valued. People who are champions of the change are supported and empowered to spread the message in a positive manner.

Above all else, a high premium is placed on timely, open and honest communications. Timely, so that rumours don't evolve into facts. Honest, so that trust is maintained.

Sugarcoating any potential pain involved in a major change helps no one. The more leaders remain upfront about the need to change and the more they express their own emotions and even voice their own reservations about the change, the greater the likelihood that people will feel trusted and that they are being told the truth.

No matter how positive the change seems on the surface, there is a bit of truth to the thinking that no one likes change, and certainly no one likes "to be changed" (anyone who has ever been married can likely attest to this truism). No matter how positive the change, there will be hardcore skeptics. It's critical not to isolate, intimidate or de-moralize the skeptics, for they can easily become anchors that drag everyone else down with them.

Instead, use the skeptics. Listen to their concerns, dig for the underlying messages. Use them as sounding boards, keeping in mind that their concerns may be legitimate. They may prove invaluable in pointing out potential pitfalls that no one else has seen. Involve them where their talents can be put to good use.

Part of the ongoing dialogue also needs to include a frank discussion as to what the negative consequences are if the status quo remains. This doesn't mean resorting to fear-mongering tactics, and it most certainly doesn't mean bullying, threatening or intimidating people into changing. But to help sell any change, people must understand that there is a cost of *not* doing things differently. Indeed, there is often a greater risk associated with *not* changing than there is with embracing a new path.

Having said all of this, remember that a key tenant of inspiring workplaces is this: Change doesn't have to be scary or chaotic. Inspiring leaders create an environment where change is viewed as a motivating challenge that everyone is inspired to take on.

What Are the Positive Consequences of Changing?

People also need to know, clearly and specifically, what the positive consequences will be of changing. Inspiring leaders need to answer the question, "Why should I bother to change?" by emphasizing the expected benefits. Don't over-promise, don't oversell, but an inspiring leader can and *should* be genuinely enthusiastic and passionate about the benefits of the change. After all, if the leaders can't get excited about it, how can anyone else be expected to?

Recognition and reward programs can help encourage people to move forward. Celebrating the small steps along the journey will help keep people motivated and instill a sense of pride in the changes taking place.

What's NOT Going to Change?

A common mistake is to focus so much time and energy on talking about all the changes taking place, that people begin to feel overwhelmed. They wonder if everything is going to change and worry that their new workplace world order will be completely unrecognizable.

Mapping out a vision of the change means clearly explaining what's staying the same, so that employees feel less uncertain, less threatened. There may be certain "untouchables" that employees are concerned about losing or changing, and letting people know that these will remain is critical. The more anchors and the more stability you can provide within the sea of change, the less rocky the boat trip will be for everyone.

What Values Will Guide the Change?

One of the constants in a workplace are your values. During a period of intense change, employees need to be reminded of these values. Leaders need to work particularly hard to embrace those values and remind employees that the core values *never* change.

What Training and Resources Will Be Available?

Too many organizations embark on a major change without the proper time or resources to fully support it. Employees need to know that training will be available to assist them and that they have somewhere to go if they have questions or need help. Senior leaders must be freed of other duties so they can spend more time communicating with employees. The more supported and cared for employees feel, the more readily they'll accept the change.

How Will the Change Be Evaluated?

In other words, "How will you know when you get there?" If employees can see progress being made, and leaders can clearly articulate what success looks like, the easier it will be for everyone to move forward. Evaluating the change can not only become a source of pride and a motivating force, it can also help appease the skeptics who need the proof in the pudding that the change really is necessary.

What if the Change Doesn't Work?

The easiest way to counter those employees who are just waiting for things *not* to work out and the easiest way to alleviate everyone's fear over the change, is to be up front and honest about any risks involved, and to clearly explain how any missteps will be handled.

Having plans in place to deal with any setbacks will obviously also help people cope with their stress.

Of course, employees also need to understand that with any change there *will* be setbacks. Mistakes *will* be made, but people will be supported throughout the process and despite the setbacks, persistence will be one of the key factors that either makes or breaks any change.

IN AN INSPIRING WORKPLACE, ONGOING CHANGE IS VIEWED AS A NECESSITY, AS A MOTIVATING FORCE AND EVEN AS A FUN CHALLENGE. DURING PERIODS OF INTENSE, MASSIVE CHANGES, THERE ARE NUMEROUS OPPORTUNITIES CREATED FOR HONEST AND TIMELY DIALOGUE AND FEEDBACK. PEOPLE ARE REWARDED FOR THEIR EFFORTS TO CHANGE, RISKS ARE CAREFULLY MANAGED AND SETBACKS ARE VIEWED AS PART OF THE PROCESS.

Inspiring Action

1. Involve employees in any major change from the very beginning to get the greatest support possible.

2. Develop a communications plan for change. Ensure there are systems set up for two-way dialogue and for information to be shared in a timely manner.

3. Create milestones and deadlines that employees can follow so they can see the progress happening. Match fun rewards or celebrations to each of the substantial milestones.

4. Make the change fun. Create a mascot, slogan or chant to accompany it. Communicate messages in fun ways by creating a newsletter or fun video or holding a monthly "talk show" format meeting with the head honchos. Create a "Top-10 Reasons To Change" list.

5. Invest the time to reinforce the workplace values that will be modelled throughout the changes.

CHAPTER 8

Inspiring Teamwork

Inspiring workplaces foster a "we" instead of "me" attitude.

Inspiring workplaces recognize the difference between a true team and a group of individuals merely pretending to function like a team with colour-coordinated baseball caps and cool t-shirts.

True *teams* in inspiring workplaces are pulled together to perform a specific task, often on a temporary basis. People from varied backgrounds are included on the team in order to draw upon a diversity of strengths, talents and experiences and to enhance creativity by incorporating a diversity of opinions and perspectives.

Inspiring workplaces understand that teams cannot be just thrown together and expected to work smoothly forevermore. Team members talk openly and honestly, not just about *what* the team is trying to accomplish but *how* the team will function together— something that is often ignored or rushed over. Guidelines for how ideas will be discussed, roles assigned, meetings managed and conflicts resolved are clearly spelled out and agreed upon.

Inspiring leaders also realize that although external motivators such as celebrations and team-building functions are important, most teams succeed or fail on the basis of how *clearly defined their goal is* and *how well each team member's roles are defined.*

Teams of people never function in a vacuum, which is why inspiring workplaces that promote a people-centred, teamwork-driven culture, create better functioning teams. While most teams might range in size anywhere from 3 to 15 people, a *culture of teamwork* is something that binds entire organizations together. It is an attitude that is pervasive in an inspiring workplace, where everyone at every level understands that part of their job is to support their coworkers. They understand that *teamwork* is a fundamental, core value and that the notion of "the whole being greater than the sum of the parts" is a key principle that any truly successful organization must be based upon.

Employees understand that, in addition to serving their external clients, they also *serve one another*. Inspiring leaders model teamwork behaviour in everything they do, because if the heads aren't cooperating, rest assured the limbs aren't either.

Inspiration from Improv

Theatre improvisation troops serve as a great model for inspiring workplace teams. Some of the rules of the road that professional theatre improvisers learn are:

Make generous offers to your fellow teammates.

Share the stage—never grandstand.

Never block ideas or suggestions.

Help the rest of your team look better.

Imagine if every workplace team functioned that way! Imagine if every team member came to the table with the attitude, "What can I do to help my fellow team members look better?" as opposed to the all too common attitude, "I will win and look better if others around me fail."

Turning Groups into Teams; Turning Me into We

First, what *prevents* teamwork in so many organizations? To name just a few of the causes of poor teamwork:

Poorly articulated organizational values.

Teamwork not being modeled at the upper levels of an organization.

Poorly defined goals that fail to emphasize teamwork.

Appraisal systems that reward acts of individualism.

Appraisal systems that fail to take into account peer opinions.

Reward and recognition systems that put too much emphasis on individual performance.

By contrast, inspiring workplaces stress the importance of teamwork in their values, going one step further by explaining just what teamwork really looks like on a day-to-day level. Teamwork, after all, is a term that means a hundred different things to a hundred different people. Inspiring workplaces use stories and examples to illustrate what teamwork actually looks like when it hits the pavement. They also talk openly about what values the concept of teamwork encapsulates and how people communicate with one another in a teamwork driven workplace.

Inspiring workplaces recognize the fact that "being a good team player" doesn't mean there *aren't* healthy disagreements and debates. Nor does being a team player imply blind loyalty to a cause or leader. Healthy teams foster honesty, openness and diversity, and whenever you mix those three elements together you're going to generate some sparks. But if you're seeking true inspiration, this is a good thing.

You can't have fire without some sparks. You can't be creative without having the ability to play around with ideas in a safe forum, and then debate and gnash your teeth over ideas once the brainstorming part of the creative process is finished. Healthy debates and disagreements ensure that everyone's ideas are being heard and being challenged. Challenged not so they can be dismissed, but challenged so that the foundation of ideas and arguments are strengthened as you move them forward.

The importance of modelling teamwork cannot be overstated. When employees hear about turf wars and personality clashes at the senior leadership table, that attitude doesn't just tend to spill over into an organization, it *floods* the workplace.

Setting goals and articulating expectations when it comes to teamwork is also essential. Equally important is to back up the importance of teamwork by ensuring employees are held accountable for their team-related behaviours and attitudes. Appraisal systems that take into account the views of co-workers help to foster a team perspective. Recognition programs that reward teams of people as well as individuals, and recognition programs that include input from front level employees also help foster a climate of positive team play.

> INSPIRING WORKPLACES EMBODY THE PRIN-
> CIPLES OF POSITIVE TEAMWORK. INSPIRING
> TEAMS ARE GIVEN THE SAME CLEAR DIREC-
> TION, GOALS, SUPPORT AND COACHING THAT
> INDIVIDUALS ARE AFFORDED.

Inspiring Action

1. Offer employees training in teamwork principles and behaviours, such as how to assign roles within a team, how to run a meeting effectively and how to resolve conflicts without lunging across the table and grabbing someone's throat.

2. Take the time to carefully select employees when putting together a team so the individual talents and abilities are matched and well-suited for the task at hand.

3. Clearly articulate the goal for any team, since this is the most important factor determining the success or failure of any team.

4. Create team rewards to encourage teamwork behaviours throughout the workplace.

CHAPTER 9

Inspiring Customer Service

Inspiring workplaces treat their employees the same way they want their employees to treat their customers.

Whether your clients are internal or external, whether you call them partners, suppliers, customers, consumers, shoppers, clients or Bob, the principles of inspiring customer service are the same. And don't for a moment think that inspiring customer service doesn't concern you, because unless you are living on the bottom of the ocean, sometime, somewhere, somehow, sooner or later, *everyone* delivers a service or product to someone else.

And the way to inspire your customers is by:

Constantly demonstrating your values.

Exceeding customer expectations.

Always answering the question:
Would you do business with you?

Constantly Demonstrate Your Values

Treat your customers with the same courtesy, respect, dignity and loyalty you expect from them. Demonstrate your core values through your actions and attitudes or risk losing your customers forever.

If you tell customers their "phone call is very important" then here's a bit of helpful advice: don't tell them so with a computer-generated voice and then put them on hold for ten minutes. When it comes to providing a service to other people, the old "actions speak louder than words" cliché rings louder than ever.

Do be careful though of falling into the old "the customer is always right" trap. It's clearly a trap, designed to stress out unsuspecting frontline staff, because the customer isn't always right. Inspiring workplaces recognize this, and although there is a high premium on service, they know that not every customer is the perfect fit for them. Moreover, they don't blindly and mindlessly side with a customer in a dispute, because they know that while it's possible that their loyal, highly trained, highly motivated employee is having a bad day, it's also possible the customer is a rude jackass who's not wanted as a customer in the first place.

But treat your true customers with loyalty and you'll get that loyalty returned. Values will increasingly take a front row seat in business, and those organizations that actively demonstrate their values consistently to their customers will stand out from the herd with inspiring service.

Exceed Expectations

We've all heard the importance of exceeding expectations time and time again. Yet, if that's the case, why do people complain that customer service has never been more *uninspiring*?

Too many organizations confuse meeting customer expectations with merely providing good customer service. The reality is though, that people *expect* a certain level of service. They *expect* the parcel to be delivered within 24 hours because that's what you told them. They *expect* your store to be open at a certain hour, they *expect* to be served promptly and courteously. Doing these things merely guarantees a neutral experience. Nothing bad happened. But nothing particularly good happened either, at least nothing to make the experience stand out; nothing to inspire loyalty or commitment from the customer.

Meeting expectations merely keeps you out of the doghouse. *It's the minimum level of service expected.* Meeting expectations is setting the bar at a nice, safe and mediocre level, and your competition couldn't be happier that's all your settling for.

Inspiring service happens when we move, at least in some small measure, above and beyond customer expectations. Inspiring service becomes the norm when we train, empower and trust employees enough to give them the creative freedom to make decisions on their own and to go the extra mile.

Inspiring service happens when organizations have inspired their employees by the way they treat and value their employees. In other words:

Happy, inspired employees = Happy, inspired customers

Given that this isn't rocket science, I am amazed at how few organizations seem to grasp this simple idea!

Inspired customers, in turn, create a positive cycle of workplace energy, since employees tend to feel more pride in what they are doing, and get treated better by the customers. The better treated they feel, the more pride they feel, the more likely they are in turn to provide better and better service.

By the way, constantly exceeding expectations doesn't have to be exhausting, and it sure doesn't have to break the bank. The great news is that once again, small is beautiful. Small gestures can produce huge payouts when it comes to inspiring customers. It can start with simply doing the small things that your competitors can't or won't.

Remember that some of the most loyal customers in the world started out having a bad experience. Inspiring workplaces know that they can turn a bad customer experience into a beautiful thing by making amends in such a way so as to wildly exceed the customer's expectations.

Decide what you mean by "good customer service" and then throw it away. Look for the simple changes in attitudes and behaviours that will raise the bar to inspire your customers, clients, co-workers or Bob, each and every time.

Would You do Business with YOU?

This question is an oldie, but it's still a goodie. Inspiring organizations ask this question all the time. And if they don't like the answer—they fix it! Inspiring workplaces are continuously looking for ideas on how to improve the service they deliver. They are constantly learning and listening to their customers, since many of their best ideas come from their customers.

Inspiring workplaces treat their customers not like walking wallets, but as *partners* in the business. They look for ways to move beyond merely offering the same old product or service and into an advisory or partnership role. And just as inspiring workplaces treat employees as people first and take care of the 24-hour person showing up at work, they treat their customers with the same consideration.

"Would you do business with you?" is a great conversation starter at a meeting or training session, as long as it's followed up by a passionate, honest discussion. Here are a few other questions to ponder in the quest for inspiring service:

What do our customers want?

No, what do they *really* want?

What do they want from us that they're getting elsewhere?

What ticks them off that we don't even know about?

What makes them smile?

What will make them tell their friends about us?

What will make them feel like they are our partners and not just our customers?

Answer these questions and your customers will be as inspired as your employees.

> INSPIRING WORKPLACES INSPIRE THEIR CUSTOMERS BY INSPIRING THEIR EMPLOYEES.

Inspiring Action

1. Take the time to hire the right people, especially when hiring people who are going to be interacting the most with real, live human beings. Hire for attitude, not skills.

2. Involve your key customers as much as possible. Include them on advisory boards, invite them to celebrations and create opportunities for ongoing feedback and input.

3. Regularly play "customer for the day" to see things through the eyes of your customers.

4. Empower (yes, I hate the word too, but it's just so darned appropriate here) your frontline employees to be able to make decisions, especially when it comes to recovering from a lousy customer service experience.

5. Offer training for frontline employees in how to inspire customers by going one step further than anyone else. Clearly define and articulate what your customer service expectations are, so that you can discuss what needs to be done to exceed those expectations to truly inspire them.

CHAPTER 10

Inspiring Creativity

Inspiring workplaces inspire innovative ideas from everyone.

Inspiring workplaces know that to be successful they need to be in the business of ideas, so creativity is a valued commodity that is hired for, nourished and rewarded.

Inspiring workplaces understand that:

Creative workspaces foster inspiration.

Creativity is a powerful motivator.

Everyone has ideas.

Ideas need to breathe.

Mistakes happen.

Creative Workspaces Foster Inspiration

In surveys the *last place* people say they come up with good ideas is the very place where people are asked to be *most creative*—the office. Employees seem to find more inspiration gardening, walking or doing household chores than they get from their workplace. The reasons that the office is seen as a place where ideas go to die include:

Stress   Dictatorial leaderships Lack of vision

Poor communication	Mundane goals
Fear of failure	Fear of making mistakes
Fear of the unknown	Fear of risk
Bureaucracy	Micromanagement
Too many rules	Committees
Stifling physical environment	An absence of fun

Now consider where people report getting most of their great ideas:

Driving	Walking	In the park
Taking a shower	Golfing	Relaxing in bed
On a hike	Riding a bike	Gardening

Why do so many people come up with ideas while undertaking these activities?

Certainly a change of scenery might be part of it. Feeling relaxed is also a large part of it. Ideas come easier when people allow their brains to meander and wander and drift and play and imagine. There is freedom in these activities, a sense of timelessness that allows the subconscious to roam and ideas to percolate.

Inspiring workplaces understand that if they want their employees to be inspired enough to imagine ideas—and lots of them—then they need to foster the kind of workplace environment, both in terms of the physical and cultural environment, that allows for freedom, a sense of playfulness and imagination.

Knowing most people come up with their best ideas away from the office leaves two possible options to boost creativity. Take your team outside for a walk in the woods when you need a little inspiration—or to a museum, park or the zoo. Anywhere that gets people away from their day-to-day worries, into a relaxed environment and into a headspace that lets the imagination breathe, changes people's perspective and lets ideas mix and mingle with other ideas.

Alternatively, the physical work environment could emulate the characteristics of these environments. A large part of fostering creativity has to do with the head space, so fostering a creative culture is clearly more important than the physical environment. However, creating a more innovative, relaxed and even playful physical environment can go a long way towards getting the creative juices flowing.

Allowing people to personalize their workspaces, adding bright colours, playful office toys and humorous props, fun signs, lots of natural lighting, plants and open spaces can help create an environment that encourages a relaxed and creative ambience. Some inspiring workplaces have even created creativity or inspiration rooms, specifically designed to help people be more playful and creative.

Creativity Is a Powerful Motivator

If you want to motivate your employees to perform at their best potential, then give them as much creative freedom over their workday as possible. Give them permission to be creative.

People want to share their ideas, so much so, that allowing employees the opportunity to be creative is one of the most powerful workplace motivators; conversely, stifling employees' creativity is one of the fastest ways of de-motivating a workforce. Employees want their ideas and input to be taken seriously, they want their ideas to be considered and responded to in a *timely manner*—even if the ideas aren't always implemented.

Part of this is allowing people to share ideas about the organization at large, but it's also simply about letting people have more say about their own destinies and jobs. It's about giving employees permission to use their creative thinking skills to solve day-to-day problems or to deal with a customer complaint using their own judgment.

Everyone Has Ideas

Not encouraging people to think, *not* providing a mechanism for capturing ideas from every individual employee and customer is tantamount to throwing money down the drain.

Inspiring workplaces know that a good idea can come from anywhere in the organization, or for that matter, from outside the workplace. Customers are often a good source for creative ideas that people too close to an issue just can't see. Inspiring workplaces create opportunities for everyone to find solutions to challenges and bring forward their ideas. Inspiring workplaces recognize that the people closest to an issue are the people most likely to spot a new idea.

Ideas Are Allowed to Breathe

One of the most common creativity killers in a workplace is preventing ideas from being brought forward, played with, tested or tried on for size. Idea-squashing language, including non-verbal signals (head shaking, rolling eyes, crossed arms) and language such as, "We've tried that before, back in 1907," is a fast and effective way to demoralize employees and smother any creative potential. Assumptions, rules, roadblocks and excuses can prematurely squash a potentially brilliant seed of an idea.

Inspiring workplaces remove the risk associated with bringing forward any new ideas because employees know that they can make suggestions *without fear of reprisal or judgment.*

Research suggests that the reason so many employees shoot down one another's ideas is because it makes them look smart. So inspiring workplaces need to foster a culture of support and trust so that people aren't rewarded for their ability to shoot down ideas, but for their ability to support and develop one another's ideas.

Seeds of ideas need to be treated as just that—*seeds* of potential, which require space, time to grow, encouragement and perhaps a little pruning to nip off the ugly parts.

Inspiring workplaces don't dismiss ideas without careful consideration. They nourish ideas, and employees use *idea-supporting* language rather than *idea-squashing* language. Inspiring workplaces realize that often the only real way to know if an idea has merit, is to try it on for size and see if it fits.

Mistakes Happen

Inspiring workplaces understand that, by definition, a truly creative idea has never been done before—by *anyone*. There are no roadmaps, guide books or "how to" manuals to show you the way. Trying out a novel idea means heading into uncharted territories, which means mistakes may happen—or even outright failure.

Inspiring workplaces have a healthy definition of failure. They view smart mistakes in the name of creativity as research, as learning opportunities, as wrong turns down a complex maze. Employees aren't punished for smart mistakes. To the contrary, in an inspiring workplace people are so strongly encouraged to try new things that occasional setbacks and flops are considered *part of the creative process of moving forward*. As the old saying goes, if you aren't making any mistakes, chances are you aren't doing anything new.

There is always an element of risk when a new idea is moved through an organization—but inspiring workplaces balance that with the notion that there is often a *greater* risk associated with *not* doing it. Inspiring workplaces accept the risk as a reality. They strive to minimize the risk of trying something new by reducing the potential consequences of failure or by minimizing the probability that something will go wrong, or both.

Small Is Still Beautiful

Inspiring workplaces don't just look for the big breakthrough idea. Instead they recognize that it's the small ideas that build momentum, that force a culture of continuous improvement and that help an organization maintain a competitive edge. Small ideas are easier to implement on a timely basis, and therefore become a wonderful motivational tool as employees actually see their ideas not only being responded to, but being implemented on an ongoing basis.

It Boils Down to Permission

The real key to unlocking employees' creative potential starts by giving people permission to be creative. Employees need to know that it is more than just okay to look for new ideas, it is *necessary*. Creating a positive, supportive culture where communication flows freely and where people are free to be themselves, are given latitude to grow, can make mistakes and try new things on for size, is the most critical element in fostering a creative work environment.

> IN AN INSPIRING WORKPLACE PEOPLE ARE INSPIRED TO BE TRULY CREATIVE.

Inspiring Action

1. Change your hiring practices to make sure you are placing a premium on creative thinking skills in the hiring process.

2. Offer training programs on creative thinking skills.

3. Create a more inspiring, fun and creative physical work environment.

4. Create an inspiration room specifically designed to encourage thinking, creativity and brainstorming.

5. Invest the time to make sure you are solving the right problem. A lot of money and effort goes into solving *symptoms* of problems, or into creating window dressing and band-aid solutions, so creative individuals and creative workplaces invest a lot of time up front making sure they are solving the real problem.

6. Practice brainstorming on a regular basis to hone people's skills and get employees used to the process. Always remind participants of the basic rules of a brainstorm, namely: there's no blocking, no judging, no hair pulling; leap frog off one another's ideas, and make the process fun to encourage spontaneity. The idea is to shoot for *quantity* of ideas over quality, recognizing that many of the ideas might be silly and completely without merit, but that going through a brainstorming process can lead to a real gem of an idea that might not have been unearthed otherwise.

7. Practice different techniques to force a change of perspective on issues such as involve people from outside the issue, change the question or problem statement, brainstorm the opposite question or use random words or stimuli to spark new connections.

8. Make your brainstorming sessions fun and encourage lots of spontaneity. Use toys and props, start the meeting with a theatre improv game or brainstorm something silly. Humour, play and laughter can lower participants' levels of stress, promote lateral thinking, level the playing field amongst participants, reframe issues and help people lower their inhibitions so that they are more likely to feel safe tossing out truly novel ideas. Keeping the discussion loose and spontaneous can also help people suggest ideas before their inner judge has a chance to prematurely censor their own ideas.

9. Create a process for *responding* to ideas on an ongoing basis in a timely and honest fashion. (Hint: *Not* responding to ideas in a timely manner is an effective way to disengage employees.)

10. Circulate a list of everyone's favourite idea-squashers ("We tried that before!") as a way of reminding employees *not* to prematurely shoot down one another's suggestions.

11. Give employees license to be creative. Include it in their goals, reward employees for their ideas and overtly tell employees that you don't just want, but that you expect, them to contribute new ideas on a regular basis. Be sure everyone knows that your workplace really does pay employees to think!

CHAPTER 11

Inspiring Work-life Balance

Inspiring workplaces treat their employees as people first, employees second.

There are two simple and vitally important reasons to take work-life balance issues seriously.

First, if a workplace's core value truly is "people come first," then offering programs that support and contribute positively to employees' personal lives and overall well-being is a *given*. Secondly, helping employees achieve balance is a selfish, bottom-line endeavour, because employees who feel more balanced *aren't* overworked. Those who are better able to meet their family commitments and personal obligations, are *less likely* to burn out. They are *less likely* to leave your organization and are *more likely* to remain healthy, productive, positive and creative.

Work-life balance will continue to be a hot topic for the foreseeable future. According to numerous surveys, balancing personal needs with increasingly stressful work demands has never been a greater priority for most employees, particularly younger employees.

While achieving true balance may be impossible, inspiring workplaces help employees achieve at least a healthier balance by offering programs such as flexible working hours, sabbaticals, telecommuting options, daycare facilities, parental leave options and even doggie daycare facilities.

A few simple principles guide the journey towards improved balance:

Set realistic workload demands.

Model a family and health first approach.

Be flexible.

Remember that work *is* personal.

Set Realistic Workload Demands

Workaholics do not produce more than others. In fact, workaholics have a tendency to encounter more health problems, more family strife, and more mental health issues. Moreover, working for long stretches without taking proper breaks increases the likelihood of mistakes, dampens creativity and, in the long run, is actually less productive. The question is this: Do you want to employ sprinters or marathon runners?

Employees need regular breaks to recharge their mental batteries and refuel their physical engines. Inspiring workplaces make sure they are not overloading their employees with unrealistic demands. They model a healthy life-work balance by ensuring that senior managers are visibly seen taking their regular vacations and working reasonable hours, so that employees don't feel pressured to become workplace martyrs.

Model a Family and Health First Approach

If you stand behind the rhetoric that employees are the most important priority, then make sure your policies reflect it. Model those values that actively demonstrate that families come first and that there is *nothing* more important than people's physical and mental health. Whenever there's a choice to be made between work and family, inspiring workplaces make sure it's clear to employees that families and health are the most important priority.

Be Flexible

Achieving work-life balance can't be done by forcing a one-size-fits-all solution onto everyone. Workplaces need to be increasingly flexible when it comes to job sharing, scheduling and assigning workloads—different employees need to be treated differently so their unique needs can be met in a reasonable manner.

Work *Is* Personal

It's a recurring theme of this book, but this seems an appropriate place to mention it again. *Uninspiring* workplaces embrace the outdated thinking that suggests one should, "Never mix business with pleasure" or that, "It's only business, don't take it personally."

Inspiring workplaces, on the other hand, believe that work is intensely personal. Work affects our health, our mental well being, our identity, self esteem, personal growth, our marriages and our family lives—*what could be more personal than all that?*

In fact, inspiring workplaces go a step further—they make sure work *is* personal. Making it personal helps ignite employees' passions, taps into their creative spirit and recognizes, once again, that it all starts and ends with real, warm-blooded human beings who do their best when their hearts are connected with their brains, and when their personal lives are balanced with their work lives.

IN AN INSPIRING WORKPLACE, WORK IS PERSONAL.

Inspiring Action

1. Set up a work-life balance committee to address common workplace concerns or issues that might affect all employees in your workplace.

2. Involve people's families through open houses, theme days and by including families in celebrations and recognition programs.

3. Make sure people take their regular breaks and vacations. A substantial percentage of workers in North America don't take the vacations they are entitled to. If workplaces are going to remain healthy, creative and inspiring, people need to know that it's *mandatory* to take their holidays because it's for everyone's benefit.

4. Create social events and regular opportunities to get to know people on a personal level, and to get to know their personal challenges, hopes and dreams.

5. Look for opportunities to encourage telecommuting wherever possible as a family-friendly, environmentally friendly and productivity-friendly alternative choice.

CHAPTER 12

Inspiring Fun

Inspiring workplaces put humour to work to create a more positive, inspiring and healthy workplace.

If you're serious about creating an inspiring workplace, then get serious about having fun. An inspiring workplace generates an environment of enthusiasm, positive energy, laughter, humour, playfulness and fun.

Not only is humour used as a powerful tool for reducing stress, improving communication, building relationships, improving customer service, sparking creativity and improving workplace morale, humour is also a barometre of workplace health. Work environments where it is easy to laugh and have fun tend to be more successful and productive workplaces.

Why Putting Humour to Work is No Joke

Too many managers and too many workplaces cling to outdated notions that stifle the use of humour on the job, sometimes because of unrealistic fears or perceptions. Inspiring workplaces understand that putting humour to work in the workplace:

Is about having a healthy sense of balance and perspective; *not* about telling jokes, being funny or being the class clown.

Is about employees taking their jobs and mission seriously, but themselves lightly.

Isn't about being unprofessional, but about using appropriate "safe" humour to be even *more* professional.

Isn't the opposite of work; it's about being a catalyst for increased productivity.

A Sense of Balance, A Sense of Perspective

Having a sense of humour is not about telling jokes, nor is it even necessarily about being funny. Having a sense of humour is about having a sense of balance and perspective about our workplace challenges and stressors. It's about how we perceive, interpret and react to the world around us; it's about finding the humour and recognizing the absurd incongruities in our day-to-day work lives. Having a sense of humour is about letting the small problems roll off our back and about learning to take ourselves lightly.

Having a healthy, positive sense of humour is largely about attitude. It's recognizing the simple truth that you have the power to choose your attitude, every day, in every work situation that you face. Inspiring workplaces understand this, and hire people that have a positive outlook to begin with. Inspiring workplaces also recognize that you have to make it *easy for people to choose a positive attitude* by creating a positive, human-centered workplace.

Take the Job Seriously, Not Yourself

There's a world of difference between taking yourself seriously and taking your job seriously. Successful people understand the difference between the two, and inspiring workplaces foster a culture that encourages people to be more successful by lightening up on themselves. Taking yourself lightly helps you manage your stress, be more creative and connect with other people more effectively.

It's Not Unprofessional

If we know that a sense of humour helps us in so many ways, then isn't it more professional to include it as a part of our repertoire of workplace skills? In fact, surveys have suggested that executives who use a healthy dose of positive humour tend to be more successful and are more likely to get promoted. As long as the humour you practice is *safe* humour: healthy, positive humour vs. destructive humour, then there's *nothing* unprofessional about sharing a sense of humour on the job.

Humour is Not the Opposite of Work

When employee morale rises, productivity rises. Happy employees = successful, productive employees. Once again, it's that simple.

After all, if humour in the workplace helps employees manage their stress, spark creative thinking, improve communication, boost morale and provide for more inspiring customer service, will that not all lead to improved productivity? Of course it will. Studies and common sense back this up time and time again. Case closed.

Don't Get Stressed—Get Funny!

Laughter truly is the best medicine when it comes to reducing workplace stress. A good laugh oxygenates the lungs, blood and brain, reduces blood pressure, relaxes tense muscles, massages internal organs to aid the digestive process, increases activity in t-killer cells that boost the immune system, reduces stress-related serum cortical and reduces the likelihood of respiratory infections by increasing the amount of salivary immunoglobin A. Yes, laughter can even make the office coffee more bearable (because, let's face it, everything tastes better when you're laughing).

One study found that several seconds of hearty laughter has the same benefit, in terms of calories lost, as a few minutes working out on a rowing machine. (Now that I know this little gem I go down to the neighbourhood gym and just laugh at the people working out.)

So adding more laughter into the workplace isn't going to kill anyone. It just might save a few lives, or at the very least, keep people healthier and less stressed.

Mentally, a healthy sense of humour is one of the most powerful stress busters available, and you don't even need an over-the-counter prescription to use it. A healthy sense of humour can help:

Mentally floss our brains so that we can focus on a problem with a clear head.

Distance us from a problem so we gain a broader perspective.

De-personalize a bad situation.

Break the tension in a stressful situation.

The reason humour can help reduce stress is two-fold. First, we need to remember that it's not the jammed photocopier, traffic jam or annoying co-worker that causes us stress; it's our *interpretation* of those situations. Our stress is created *solely* by what our brains and bodies are telling us about the challenges facing us.

Secondly, although there are literally hundreds of things we have no control over in our work life, we all have 100 percent control over our *reaction* to any situation. Not 87 percent. Not even 98.5 percent. 100 percent.

So humour lets us reframe our interpretation to reduce our stress. It gives us the option of choosing a different reaction, and thereby empowering us, in the face of a stressful situation.

The Three R's of Humour

To tap into your sense of humour in a stressful situation, inspiring workplaces need to encourage their employees to practice the R's of humour:

Reward.

Reframe.

Relax.

Reward

We've talked about how important it is to reward ourselves and others as a way to reinforce positive behaviour, but sometimes we need a reward when things *don't* go as planned. After all, when is humour most needed? When can an injection of fun be most beneficial?

Search and rescue dogs that are sniffing out nothing but corpses in a huge disaster have been known to become so depressed that they stop working. So rescue officials will sometimes bury a live member of the team in the avalanche or debris so that the dog gets rewarded in a positive manner for its efforts. Call me crazy, but I'm thinking that if it works with dogs, it might work with humans, too.

By attaching fun rewards, or giving people a "humour break" when things go badly, you can lift spirits and break the cycle of stress. For example, offering employees a fun perk for having the "Customer from Hell" experience of the month is just one simple way to reward a common workplace stressor.

Reframe

Take a page from comedians and mentally reframe the situation to find the humour in it. Force yourself to find the good or better still, the humorous, in a bad situation. Exaggerate wildly to find some humour. Ask yourself what, in a year's time, will you find funny about the situation? Put yourself in someone else's shoes to find the humour. Or tell yourself, "It could always be worse" and then wildly exaggerate the possibilities until you can't help but laugh.

The reframing power of humour is also a powerful catalyst for creative thinking. Humour, by changing our lens on a situation, can lead people to unearth wonderful new insights and creative ideas.

Relax

Remember the therapeutic benefits of humour and laughter and simply take a humour break. Go visit your newly minted "Humour Room," find a co-worker and implore them to make you laugh, read your favourite cartoon book, play with a funny prop or put on a goofy hat. Just do something that shakes out the cobwebs and breaks you away from the routine, after all, as the late Milton Berle once said, "Laughter is an instant vacation."

Communicating with Humour

Inspiring workplaces understand the power of humour to transform uninspiring company reports, meetings and business presentations into inspiring forms of communication that keep people awake, and engage and inform the audience in a more open, honest and effective manner. Research suggests that when a message is wrapped in humour, people retain as much as 700 percent more of the information, and people are five times more likely to comply with a request or regulation.

Yet, how often do uninspiring leaders fall into the trap of thinking that somehow they are being effective by droning on with vague and often insulting jargon-speak, mind-numbing pie charts and lifeless text devoid of emotion or any sense of personality?

If you want to inspire people to action, then look for as many ways as possible to connect people's hearts with their minds, to engage people intellectually and emotionally, with the power of humour.

Leading with Laughter

Business author Paul Hawken said it best: "We lead by being human. We do not lead by being corporate, by being professional or by being institutional." Leading with self-effacing humour can help build trust in a workplace environment, tear down walls and create an atmosphere conducive to honest dialogue and creativity.

Putting Humour to Work without Getting Fired

As I suggested earlier, applying humour in the workplace successfully means you need to practice "safe" humour—

humour that breaks down walls, brings people together and laughs *with,* not at people. Safe workplace humour needs to be respectful of the:

Timing of the humour.

Audience.

Topic.

Remember, you can be as gross, cutting, sarcastic and politically incorrect with your humour as you want when you're with your friends and family. But in an inspiring workplace setting, it's simply common sense that people need to be respectful of differences in one another's perspectives. So know your audience, whether it's an audience of one or 1,000, and avoid religious, sexist, racist and ethnic humour of any kind.

Relevant Humour Gets the Last Laugh

Ideally, if you can integrate or incorporate fun and humour into your everyday work activities, then work no longer feels like work. Turn a boring, mundane task into a game and watch productivity soar—not to mention, your creativity and mood.

The more relevant to your workplace the type of humour you share and indulge in, the more resonance it will have with employees. Relevant humour becomes a wonderful bonding tool and a way to create a sense of history and tradition in your workplace.

Listen Between the Punch Lines

Employees in an inspiring workplace, should, in theory at least, have a tough time finding the humour in most Dilbert cartoons, because for humour to work there should be at least a morsel of truth buried inside it. Which means that when employees practice subversive, sarcastic or unhealthy workplace humour, inspiring leaders should be listening for the meaning behind the laughter, and use that humour to their advantage to learn about workplace issues that employees may only feel comfortable speaking up about under the cloak of humour.

Once Again, Small Is Beautiful

When it comes to practicing workplace humour and fostering a lighter atmosphere, small gestures done on a consistent basis make the world of difference. In fact, studies suggest that most workplace humour happens spontaneously. Once again it simply comes down to giving people permission to be themselves, to be human and to put humour to work.

> INSPIRING WORKPLACES FOSTER A POSITIVE ATMOSPHERE FILLED WITH LAUGHTER, LIFE, PLAY AND HUMOUR.

Inspiring Action

1. Start a "Humour Squad" to look for creative ways to build humour into your workplace on a regular basis.

2. Create a Humour Room or "Lighten up!" room where stressed out employees can unwind.

3. Create a humour library and stockpile it with humour books, audio CDs and DVDs.

4. Create a "Humour Code of Conduct" to send the message that safe, positive humour is strongly encouraged and welcomed in your workplace. Make the Humour Code of Conduct *fun,* not something that sounds like it came from a committee of lawyers at head office.

5. Create a humour bulletin board where employees can post and share humorous items.

6. Start a humour file or book to capture relevant humour found in your workplace.

7. Hold an annual fun awards event and dole out humorous awards such as, the Person Most Likely to O.D. on Caffeine Award.

8. Create your own offbeat theme days and holidays.

9. Create a "Humour First Aid Kit" for the office and stockpile it with funny props, costume parts, books and wacky photos—anything that employees can use to access their sense of humour and de-stress with in the event of a "serious" emergency.

10. Include a "humour break" in your meeting agendas.

11. Offer humour in the workplace training to encourage people to develop their humour skills in an appropriate manner.

CHAPTER 13

Parting Thoughts

I'll keep this short and sweet.

Life is short. Life is really, really short and when you're dead, you're going to be dead for a very, very long time.

Work plays an enormously powerful role in this short journey called life. You deserve (at least in my humble opinion) to work in a workplace that is passionate, fun, engaging, caring, respectful, humane and truly inspiring. Your customers deserve it. Your community deserves it. Your friends and families deserve it.

So do something **today** that takes your workplace at least one step closer towards true inspiration.

CHAPTER 14

Inspiring Workplaces Resources

The Humour at Work Institute™ offers training workshops ranging from one hour keynote presentations to full-day workshops in the following topics:

Inspiring Workplaces

Putting Humour to Work

Putting Creativity to Work

Inspiring Ideas for Inspiring Presentations
(Presentation Skills)

The Humour at Work Institute™ also offers a variety of humour at work resources:

Putting Humour to Work Training DVD

Turn Monday Into Funday! Meeting-opener DVD

You Can't Be Serious! Putting Humour to Work
(book)

Putting Humour to Work audio CDs

Putting Humour to Work memory cards
(boost your humour tips)

What's So Funny About Alberta?
(book)

When Do You Let the Animals Out?
(book)

For more information, to book a program or to order a product:

Website: www.MikeKerr.com

E-mail: mike@mikekerr.com

Phone: 1-866-609-2640
(Monday – Friday, 9:00 a.m. – 5:00 p.m. MST)
(Weather permitting—if it's really nice out, who knows where we'll be?)

CHAPTER 15

Inspiring Workplaces Reading List

This list is by no means comprehensive, but I wanted to offer a starter menu of a few books that can offer further guidance, ideas and inspiration. (You might especially want to check out "You CAN'T Be Serious! Putting Humor to Work" by some guy named Michael Kerr—apparently it's packed full of great ideas and fabulous humour.)

1,001 Ways to Energize Employees, by Bob Nelson. Workman Publishing, 1997.

1,001 Ways to Reward Employees, by Bob Nelson. Workman Publishing, 1994.

Care Packages for the Workplace, by Barbara A. Glanz. McGraw-Hill, 1996.

First, Break All the Rules: What the World's Greatest Managers Do Differently, by Marcus Buckingham and Curt Coffman. Simon and Schuster, 1999.

Good to Great: Why Some Companies Make the Leap . . . And Others Don't, by Jim Collins. HarperBusiness, 2001.

Harvard Business Review on Motivating People, Harvard Business School Press, 2003.

Harvard Business Review on Work and Life Balance, Harvard Business School Press, 2000.

Inspire! What Great Leaders Do, by Lance Secretan. John Wiley and Sons, 2004

Joy at Work, by Dennis W. Bakke. PVG, 2005.

Love 'Em or Lose 'Em: Getting Good People to Stay, by Beverly Kaye and Sharon Jordan-Evans. Berret-Koehler Publishers, 2002.

Love It, Don't Leave It: 26 Ways to Get What You Want at Work, by Beverly Kaye and Sharon Jordan-Evans. Berret-Koehler Publishers, 2003.

Nuts! Southwest Airlines' Crazy Recipe for Business and Personal Success, by Kevin and Jackie Freiberg. Bard Press, 1996.

Return on Imagination, by Tom Wujec and Sandra Muscat. Prentice Hall, 2002.

Sacred Cows Make the Best Burgers: Developing Change-Ready People and Organizations, by David Brandt. Warner Books, 1996.

The One Thing You Need to Know, by Marcus Buckingham. Free Press, 2005.

The Seven-Day Weekend: Changing the Way Work Works, by Ricardo Semler. Portfolio, 2004.

Why Business People Speak Like Idiots, by Brian Fugere, Chelsea Hardaway, & Jon Warshawsky. Free Press, 2005

Why Pride Matters More than Money, by Jon R. Katzenbach. Crown Business, 2003.

You CAN'T Be Serious! Putting Humor to Work, by Michael Kerr, Humour at Work Institute™. Speaking of Ideas, 2001, 2004. (1-866-609-2640)